STRATEGIC AIRPORT
PLANNING

This book will explore a new approach to airport planning that better captures the complexities and velocity of change in our contemporary world. As a result, it will lead to higher performing airports for users, business partners, investors and other stakeholders. This is especially pertinent since airports will need to come back better from the Covid-19 pandemic.

The book explains the importance of articulating a clear strategy, based on a rigorous analysis of the competitive landscape while avoiding the pitfalls of ambiguity and 'virtue signalling'. Having done so, demand forecasts can be developed that resemble S-curves, not simple straight lines, that reflect strategic opportunities and threats from which a master plan can be developed to allocate land and capital in a way that maximizes return on assets and social licence. The second distinctive feature of this book is the premise that planning an airport as an island, a fortress even, does not work anymore given how interconnected airports are with other components of the transportation system, the economies and communities they serve and the rapid pace of social and technological change. In summary, the book argues that airport planning needs to move beyond its traditional boundaries.

The book is replete with real examples from airports of all sizes around the world and includes practical advice and tools for executives and managers. It is recommended reading for individuals working in the airport business or the broader air transport industry, members of airports' board of directors, who may be new to the business, elected officials, policy makers and urban planners in jurisdictions hosting or adjacent to airports, regulators, economic development professionals and, finally, students.

Mike Brown has 35 years of experience in the airport industry and has completed strategic plans, master plans and economic impact assessments at Canada's two largest airports, Toronto Pearson and Vancouver International, amongst others, and has a track record of innovation, analytical rigour and successful execution. Mike is currently Honorary Senior Research Fellow in the Transport Strategy Centre at Imperial College, London, where he works with nine global hub airports on improving business performance.

MANAGING AVIATION OPERATIONS

Series Editor: Peter J. Bruce
Associate Editor: John M. C. King

The purpose of this series is to provide a comprehensive set of materials dealing with the key components of airline and airport operations. To date, this innovative approach has not been evident among aviation topics and certainly not applied to operational areas of airlines or airports. While more recent works have begun, in brief, to consider the various characteristics of operational areas, the *Managing Aviation Operations* series will expand coverage with far greater breadth and depth of content.

Airlines and airports are devoid of specific topic knowledge in ready-made, easy-to-read, creditable resources. Tapping into industry expertise to drive a range of key niche products will resource the industry in a way not yet seen in this domain. Therefore, the objective is to deliver a collection of specialised, internationally sourced and expertly written books to serve as readily accessible guides and references primarily for professionals within the industry. The focus of the series editors will be to ensure product quality, user readability and appeal, and transparent consistency across the range.

Airline Operations Control
Peter J. Bruce and Chris Mulholland

Aviation Leadership
The Accountable Manager
Mark Pierotti

Strategic Airport Planning
Mike Brown

For more information about this series, please visit: www.routledge.com/Aviation-Fundamentals/book-series/MAO

STRATEGIC
AIRPORT
PLANNING

MIKE BROWN

LONDON AND NEW YORK

Cover image: © Getty Images

First published 2022
by Routledge
4 Park Square, Milton Park, Abingdon, Oxon OX14 4RN

and by Routledge
605 Third Avenue, New York, NY 10158

Routledge is an imprint of the Taylor & Francis Group, an informa business

© 2022 Mike Brown

British Library Cataloguing-in-Publication Data
A catalogue record for this book is available from the British Library

Library of Congress Cataloging-in-Publication Data
A catalog record has been requested for this book

ISBN: 978-1-032-00237-8 (hbk)
ISBN: 978-1-032-00235-4 (pbk)
ISBN: 978-1-003-17326-7 (ebk)

DOI: 10.4324/9781003173267

Typeset in Galliard
by codeMantra

I would like to dedicate this book to the memory of Dr Michael Williams, Sir Walter Raleigh Fellow and Tutor in Geography at Oriel College, Oxford who first taught me about S-curves, Michael O' Brien, formerly Vice President, Strategy at Vancouver Airport Authority and Michael Matthews, Project Director, 2027 Vancouver International Airport Master Plan, for teaching me the craft of strategic and master planning and finally Howard Eng, former President and Chief Executive Officer of the Greater Toronto Airports Authority, for giving me the opportunity to hone those skills at Toronto Pearson.

CONTENTS

CONTENTS

FIGURES

TABLES

ACKNOWLEDGEMENTS

I'm grateful for the assistance and guidance of my two editors, Peter Bruce and John King, Greg Fordham, Principal of AirBiz, for making the initial introductions, Kerr Lammie and Martin Lephoron of AirBiz too for their suggestions, Mike Webber for his helpful comments on the cargo chapter and Paul Cheng from the Airport Authority of Hong Kong for his help on understanding the Pearl River Delta catchment area. Finally, I am indebted to Peta Wolmarans, Director of Planning at Vancouver Airport Authority, for her peer review.

1

WHY PLAN?

How to Build an Airport

In 1946, the Government of Canada started assembling land for a second, north runway at Vancouver International Airport, Canada. That runway opened 50 years later in 1996 after decades of land assembly, expropriation, litigation, community opposition and a formal environmental impact assessment. When it did go into service, it was restricted to arrivals only, with a few exceptions. Frankfurt Airport's fourth runway first appeared in a Master Plan in 1997 and it opened 14 years later, with operating restrictions, while Amsterdam Schiphol's fifth runway, the 'Polderbaan', was 18 years between planning and the first aircraft landing on it. Meanwhile, Heathrow's third, northern runway is not scheduled to open until 2030 having first being announced as government policy in 2009.

Passenger terminals can have long gestation periods too. London Heathrow's Terminal 5 was first mooted in 1982 and finally opened 26 years later in 2008.

In some cases, it can take less time to build a completely new airport than add a runway or terminal to an existing one, especially if there is a greenfield site and approvals and permits are expedited. Dubai's Al Maktoum International Airport opened in 2010, five years after it was first conceived. The new Istanbul Airport was announced in 2012; the construction of the airport started in 2015 and was opened fully in 2019.

Berlin's Brandenburg Airport (BER) opened on October 31, 2020, 14 years after construction started and 20 years after official planning was launched.

DOI: 10.4324/9781003173267-1

IMMOVABLE OBJECTS AND IRRESISTIBLE FORCES

What makes airport planning challenging is that it's where irresistible force of the demand for air transportation meets the science of aeronautics which ordains that we need immovable long, straight and flat pieces of concrete, free of obstacles at each end, to launch and land aircraft. Figure 1.1 shows the accelerating rate of growth in air travel, pre-pandemic.

Airports rightly and necessarily devote considerable time and energy to planning their investments to ensure they are the right ones, at the right time and in the right place. All that remains true, but the theme of this book is about how we need to cast a wider net in this process, beyond the traditional boundaries of airport planning. Why? Airports themselves are becoming 'distributed' in that lots of things we used to do at the airport, like checking in or shopping, we now do from home or in an Uber on our way to the airport. They are also part of larger air transport ecosystem which includes aircraft and air navigation and are magnets in their metropolitan areas shaping land values and uses in their immediate vicinity but also for many miles beyond. Planning an airport as an island, a fortress even, does not work anymore.

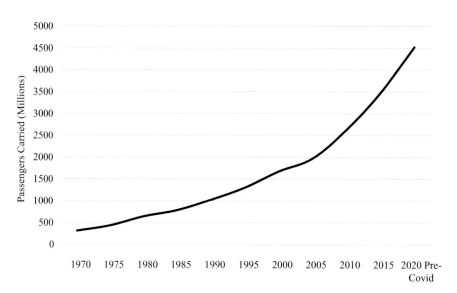

Figure 1.1 Global Demand for Air Travel.

Source: International Civil Aviation Organization, Civil Aviation Statistics of the World and ICAO staff estimates.

By any definition, the airport industry is a capital intensive one, that is, the amount of capital required to generate $1 of revenue is high and much more than the amount of labour. Based on a sample of 126 airports, the average capital intensity was $8.39 in total assets per dollar of revenue in 2015.[1] In contrast, labour costs were only $0.23 per dollar of revenue.

Planning is important not only because of the quantity of capital consumed by airports but also because of the characteristics of that capital. First, it's very long-lived. Terminal buildings and runways are not pop-up structures but substantial ones that must be 'built to last' to minimize the risks of physical and functional obsolescence. Second, it's immobile, so cannot be disassembled and relocated to a new and growing market, in contrast with airlines whose capital assets are ultimately mobile. Third, it's very difficult to build a modular runway, so airport capital tends to be monolithic or 'lumpy'. Fourth, it's not easily transferable in the way that a regular office building could be converted into shops, a hotel or apartments. Finally, it has externalities because the aircraft that arrive and depart on a runway create noise and emissions that can negatively affect surrounding communities. This last point leads us to the other reason to plan: maintaining social licence, defined[2] as broad public support for the airport's strategy and the major infrastructure projects that flow from it.

It is reasonable to say that social licence is difficult to earn requiring years, if not decades, of transparency, engagement and openness, as well as clear and consistent messaging on the benefits that the airport confers. As hard as it is to gain, social licence can be very easily lost but undeniably its importance will be magnified as the industry recovers from the pandemic. Arguably to retain and rebuild their social licence, airports will have to come back: cleaner, greener, leaner and keener.

- **Cleaner** as in Covid sanitation protocols will outlast the pandemic;
- **Greener** in that concern about the impact of air travel on climate change has not gone away plus the collective sense of achievement in conquering Covid will spill over into renewed vigour in tackling emissions;
- **Leaner** in that margins will be under pressure because our customers expect continuous improvement in processes and 'virtual' represents real competition; and
- **Keener** in terms of being even more actively engaged in the community's economic and social well-being, for example, working to repair some of the socio-economic inequities that the pandemic has exposed.

THE PYRAMID OF PLANNING

'Planning' is a big, generic term, so it can be helpful to break it down into five interlinked levels each with different time horizons and levels of granularity. Think of it as a Pyramid of Planning (see Figure 1.2) and an aid to successful execution.

At the top level, there is a strategic plan. This is not where specific projects are itemized but instead articulates the business strategy of the airport based on assessment of the competitive landscape. It says: 'we have looked at the options available to us and this is the airport we intend to be'. Spoiler alert: many airports fudge this part of the process and end up trying to be all things to all people.

A Master Plan is the next level down on the Pyramid of Planning and is a document with typically a 20-year time horizon that takes that demand forecast and translates into the land and facilities necessary to accommodate it. Most airports have a Master Plan because it is a legislated requirement but regardless it's just good business practice.

Below the Master Plan sits two sets of ten-year plans: a capital and financial plan which takes the major investments identified in the

Figure 1.2 Pyramid of Planning.

Source: Vancouver Airport Authority, modified by author.

Master Plan and turns them into discrete projects with more accurate cost estimates and a series of sub-area development plans that specify servicing, development options and uses in more detail. This is the link between a broad recommendation in the Master Plan, for example, the requirement to add ten international gates, into a specific project which will need to be designed, funded and approved. For land zoned generically as 'airside commercial' in the master plan, a sub-area plan can be developed for various precincts such as air cargo, business aviation or aircraft maintenance. Without these linking plans, a Board of Directors can be faced with a series of projects or developments to approve but without a clear idea of how they related back to the Master Plan and the strategy.

The bottom two layers of the pyramid are multi-year and one-year operating plans and budgets. The multi-year version can have a horizon of two to five years as it usually takes this long for any operational or commercial project to cycle through the phases of conception, planning, testing and implementation.

The point is that linking the five tiers of planning increases the probability of synchronizing the airport's strategy with the operating plan for the current year. It would be a mistake to underestimate the forces that can cause a misalignment, which can include miscommunication, misunderstanding, conflicting incentives, 'pet' projects, ones that are ill-conceived or those with powerful advocates. For example, an airport makes a strategic choice to reduce greenhouse gas emissions; yet in another part of the organization, negotiations are underway to lease a piece of orphaned land to a used-car dealership.

SUMMARY AND CONCLUSIONS

Airport planning has never been more challenging, nor more important. It is really a risk management exercise. It is really a risk management exercise, that is, minimizing the possibility of building underperforming assets and losing social licence. Arguably these risks are much higher with societal disquiet about aviation's impact on climate change, the pace of technological development, the emergence of new business models and the Covid-19 pandemic. The antidote to this challenge is to take airport planning beyond its traditional boundaries to capture a broader set of influences, deploy new frameworks and adopt different ways of thinking.

Notes

1. Author's calculation.
2. Gunster and Neubauer, "From Public Relations".

Bibliography

Gunster, Shane, and Robert Neubauer. "From Public Relations to Mob Rule: Media Framing of Social Licence in Canada". *Canadian Journal of Communication* 43, no. 1 (2018): 11–32. https://doi.org/10.22230/cjc.2018v43n1a3342.

2   STRATEGIC PLANNING

INTRODUCTION

Strategic planning conjures up visions of war rooms where grand plans are hatched and executed or, in a corporate setting, a two-day meeting at a country resort where the company's strategy is hammered out with the aid of a facilitator and large Post-It notes plastered on the conference room walls.

Strategy is about choice, of the difficult and sometimes controversial variety and, yes, you can and should decide what kind of airport you want to be. For example, some small airports will desperately hang on to their one daily scheduled service, bearing all the fixed costs of a passenger terminal and fire fighting capabilities as a matter of civic pride rather than a rational strategy.

THE STRATEGIC TRILEMMA

A trilemma is a triangle of desired outcomes, only two of which are possible. We find them in business, politics, economics and the environment.

The most common strategic trilemma in business is: 'fast, cheap and good'. A company can offer a fast and good service, for example, the guaranteed overnight package delivery services of FedEx or UPS, but it is not cheap. Or it can offer cheap and good service, which means that the package will be delivered intact but not by a specific date or time, so a reasonable characterization of regular postal service. Finally, there may be a service offering that is fast and cheap but not very good, meaning the package may be damaged in transit, the tracking system is non-existent or you must collect your item at a distant and dingy depot.

Another example comes from human resources. In many companies' performance management systems for senior staff, a high performing

DOI: 10.4324/9781003173267-2

employee is described as somebody who gets things done, demonstrates creativity and innovation as well as being a great team player and leader. While such individuals undoubtedly exist, most people only check two out of the three boxes. If we get things done and are great team players and leaders, we may not be the most innovative because that sometimes means stepping on a few toes or bending some rules. On the other hand, if we are great innovators and we get things done too, we may march to a slightly different drum than the rest of the team. Finally, if we are great team players and leaders and scoring highly on creativity and innovation, we may struggle to deliver on the basics.

In the field of energy, the trilemma is the trade-off between affordable, secure and sustainable. For example, conventional kerosene is affordable and secure because it's the incumbent aviation fuel with a global supply chain but its greenhouse gas (GHG) emissions means it does not check the sustainability box. In contrast, bio-aviation fuels (BAF) are sustainable but not particularly secure, as production capacity is small and BAF costs anywhere between two and eight times as much as kerosene.

Many airports have legacy crosswind runways which were built for an era when aircraft were smaller. Particularly at large international airports, these runways are only used on an exception basis, but they occupy or sterilize valuable land which could be deployed to expand the passenger terminal building or for other commercial uses. A strategic trilemma arises because the goal of becoming a global hub, and the revenue needed to finance that, conflicts with a tradition of allowing small aircraft to land in all wind conditions.

THE PERILS OF STRATEGIC BLUNTNESS

In his book *Good Strategy, Bad Strategy*[1] Richard Rumelt, a professor at the Anderson School of Business at UCLA, argues that good strategy has a kernel that is made up of a diagnosis, a guiding policy and a coherent series of actions. Essentially, the strategic planning process starts with an honest and correct diagnosis of the problems that if unchecked can threaten the long-term viability of the enterprise. Bad strategy, on the other hand, contains 'fluff' or noble words, fails to identify and face the real challenge, and only offers aspirational statements.

Using Rumelt's framework, an airport could decide that the biggest threat to its long-term viability is the issue of climate change. The guiding policy could be to achieve net zero emissions in ten years, and then the coherent set of actions would be a series of investments, partnerships, pricing and operational changes to reach that goal. This is not to say that other goals, such as offering good customer service, are unimportant, just that they do not form existential threats to the enterprise.

Unrecognized or unacknowledged trilemmas are often at the root of a faulty diagnosis and the strategic bluntness that follows. Let's start with the example of Austin-Bergstrom International Airport (AUS) in Austin, Texas which decided in 2008 to open a low-cost terminal (LCT). At the time, a low-cost carrier, VivaAerobus from Mexico, wanted to enter the market but did not need the full-service offering, or the rates and charges, at Austin's main passenger terminal. The attraction for airports is that low-cost carriers can stimulate passenger demand significantly and if they can be accommodated at little or no marginal cost, a low-cost carrier can be very profitable. An abandoned US Air Force warehouse was retrofitted to very basic standards to create an LCT; passengers walked across the ramp to and from the aircraft and the baggage delivery system was a simple roller belt. The biggest challenge according to Austin Airport officials was not operating two physically separate terminals or creating a new set of fees and charges for the LCT. It was that airport staff who were steeped in a full-service culture had difficulty suddenly taking that hat off and doffing a low cost one, sometimes in the middle of a shift. Eventually Austin Airport put the LCT under the control of a different management company where a legitimate low-cost culture could take root.

Another example of strategic bluntness is the secondary airport that aspires to compete with the major hub in a metropolitan area, often driven by municipal pride. A key question is why a major international carrier would defect from the global hub's supporting ecosystems of fuel, catering, ground handling, not to mention the flows of connecting passengers, to establish a station at the secondary airport? An alternative strategy would be to serve the low-cost origin-destination market and possibly attract some aerospace businesses looking for affordable land.

Given the capital-intensive nature of the airport business, the need for strategic clarity in the planning and design of facilities is of the utmost importance; yet many airports stumble around blindly here. The most common planning and design guidelines actually come from its customers, the air carriers' industry association (IATA). It lays out a series of Levels of Service (LOS)[2] for building size and processes. The levels of service range from A to E. Most airports default to LOS C, as one tends to do when presented with a five-point scale[3] and that's probably not an unreasonable target for a mature industry serving an affluent clientele. But it needs to be an explicit choice.

Suppose an airport wants to distinguish itself by offering a better level of service. Possibly it serves a predominantly business market or an affluent leisure one, for example, Bermuda (BDA). If we look at the differences in space per passenger between LOS B and C, it is 19% more on average[4] which is material. The business case would need to demonstrate that the incremental revenue stream from relaxed customers with more time to shop and dine is worth the additional capital and operating costs.

Similarly, an airport may see its niche as serving price-sensitive, leisure travellers and deliberately opt to be 'cheap and cheerful' in which case the capital and operating costs at LOS D will be about 23% lower than at LOS C. Again, these are not trivial choices but being explicit about them makes the strategy sharper and the master plan more effective.

Clearly the post-pandemic world will likely see the adoption of different space standards and, as we will see later, the increasing incidence of mobility impairments in an ageing population will change them too.

There's no reason why standards could not be adopted from outside the airport world, for example, shopping malls, sports stadia or other mass entertainment venues.

The airline industry gives us many examples of the perils of strategic bluntness. Ted was a low-cost carrier set up by United Airlines in 2004, within the corporate structure of United. Other examples are Delta's Song and Air Canada's Tango. As somebody said 'Ted is the end of United'; that did not prove to be the case, but Ted was folded up in 2009 partly due to a spike in oil prices but also because of the challenges of grafting a new corporate culture onto an existing one, as we saw at Austin Airport. Start-up companies tend to have cultures that 'move fast, break things, have fun and make money' which is the antithesis of an established corporation. The old, dominant culture can easily smother it.[5] That's one of the reasons why the most successful low-cost carriers in the world such as Southwest Airlines and Ryanair started life that way and have not deviated. As Michael O'Leary, the CEO of Ryanair, once said that his corporate strategy was simple: 'pile it high and sell it cheap'.

It's entirely reasonable for an airport to opt for 'good and fast' but many then make the mistake of adding 'to be the lowest cost' or 'most cost efficient' to the list of strategic objectives, which just muddies the water.

Hopefully having made the case for strategic clarity, we should look at the playing field.

When we talk about 'beyond the boundaries', we are referring to two types: the geographical kind and the functional kind.

The geographical boundaries speak for themselves; airports have significant effects on land use around them and planning in isolation can result in missed opportunities. Airports have catchment areas,[6] the boundaries of which are sometimes difficult to discern but, as a general rule, expanding them is better for business than having them contract. Finally, tasks we used to do at the airport now happen elsewhere, as the rapid adoption of online check-in shows, so the airport as a 'place' is becoming distributed. We're quickly moving the parameters of airport planning to home-to-home.

What is a functional boundary? Think of any transportation system as having three component parts: the terminal, the vehicle and the way, so, respectively, in aviation, airports, aircraft and air navigation. Throughout this book, we will see examples of how changes in one component impact the others; for example, when Russia and China opened their airspace in the late 1990s, it allowed aircraft to fly shorter, polar routes between North America and Asia. This saved time, fuel and emissions and made trans-Pacific service to secondary airports commercially viable, changing the competitive landscape for the traditional coastal gateways. Long-range, narrow-body aircraft make viable routes between eastern North America and Europe that were previously too thin to support non-stop service. To use another example, when air navigation authorities change the design of airspace, it often results in neighbourhoods that previously heard very little aircraft noise suddenly being exposed to a lot more of it. The airport, with its high public profile and noise complaint line, inevitably feels the brunt of this and the mitigation of these impacts sometimes results in sub-optimal runway use.

STRATEGIC TEMPLATES

How does an airport work through these issues systematically to formulate a strategic plan? There is a lot to consider.

SWOT

This is the grandfather of strategic templates and the default that many airports reach for. Simple and intuitive, all you need is a piece of paper and then draw four quadrants on it. The basic idea is that the strengths and weaknesses are focused on the company while the opportunities and threats are external. An example is provided in Figure 2.1.

Strengths	Weaknesses
Strong Brand Experienced Leadership Team	Low Engagement Scores Board-Senior Leadership Team Relationships
Opportunities	**Threats**
Export Markets Expanded on-line presence.	Cyber Attacks New Disruptors

Figure 2.1 Sample SWOT Analysis.
Source: Author.

In the hands of a skilled facilitator, SWOT can be helpful but unguided; companies tend to overstate strengths and underplay weaknesses because in a corporate boardroom, it can be hazardous to be too vocal about the organization's shortcomings. The enumeration of opportunities and challenges tends to suffer a similar fate: opportunities are over-egged while threats get downplayed. In other words, this harks back to Richard Rumelt's admonition that a hard-headed diagnosis of the problem is the start of an effective strategic plan, but companies can find it difficult to be honest with themselves.

A SWOT analysis is a necessary but not sufficient condition for strategy development. It gets the issues on the table and provides a reasonable inventory of the airport's situation at a point in time. However, it does not usually weight or rank the factors, for example, is the threat from intense competition orders-of-magnitude more serious than fuel price volatility or only marginally so?

A more rigorous approach needs to be taken, particularly with respect to the opportunities and threats. A deeper dive is needed and for that we turn to Michael Porter's Five Competitive Forces.

PORTER'S FIVE COMPETITIVE FORCES

Michael Porter is a professor at Harvard Business School and has a useful template for any company to assess the competitive forces arrayed against it (Porter, 1998). The advantage of Porter's framework is a more systematic treatment of threats and opportunities identified in a SWOT analysis. Porter argues that there are five competitive forces: the bargaining power of customers, the bargaining power of suppliers, existing competitors, new entrants and, finally, substitutes for your product or services.

BARGAINING POWER OF CUSTOMERS

If you have a single customer that accounts for 80% of your revenue, they have considerable bargaining power in your relationship. Obviously, this power is mediated through the options your big customer has which are probably limited in the short run, for example, Delta Airlines is not going to dismantle its hub at Atlanta (ATL) overnight. It can however exercise power in other ways, for example, by deploying new aircraft at other hubs, withholding approval for capital spending or by lobbying, publicly and privately, to reverse decisions it believes are not in its best interest. An example of the latter would be the opposition by Alaska Airlines, the dominant and mainly domestic air carrier at Seattle-Tacoma International Airport (SEA), to a proposed new international terminal.

BARGAINING POWER OF SUPPLIERS

If there is a specific input you need to run your business, and there are no viable alternatives in the short term, that supplier has bargaining power over you. For example, in the 1980s, the Japanese steel industry strategically increased its choice of coal suppliers by encouraging the development of mines in Canada and Australia, often with government subsidies. Likewise, US airlines welcomed Airbus and Embraer to the market because it reduced their dependence on Boeing.

In the case of airports, the monopoly suppliers are the government agencies policing the border, providing air traffic control services or preboard screening. After all, airports are just international borders with planes around them. If an airport is unhappy with staffing levels at international arrivals, it can hardly go to another supplier. Likewise, if an airport is dissatisfied with the number of air traffic controllers on duty on a busy, summer weekend because it is reducing runway capacity, there are no alternative vendors.

A good example of the failure to appreciate the bargaining power of a sole supplier comes from the field of cargo building development. Passenger terminals are usually built and operated by the airport authority but facilities for cargo have, in most cases, been developed by private companies, on behalf of end-users like FedEx or UPS that want to prioritize their capital spending on aircraft and software, not bricks and mortar. Likewise, private developers build and operate multi-tenant cargo buildings that accommodate smaller firms in the customs broker and freight forwarder community, clusters that are sometimes referred to as a 'cargo village'.

Starting in the 1990s, many airports started to focus on their contribution to the economic well-being of their community and, with globalization and international supply chains, wanted to understand the cargo business better. Some third-party developers resisted this encroachment into 'their business' and relationships became strained. This was not a good strategic choice for the developers because, at the end of the day, the airport is the sole supplier of airport land. In any event, many options for airports and developers to collaborate existed, for example, the airport could contribute the land as equity in a joint venture as opposed to passively leasing it.

CURRENT COMPETITORS

An airport may have several competitors in different lines of business: origin-destination passengers, connecting ones and cargo.

The four main hubs in Europe: London Heathrow (LHR), Paris Charles de Gaulle (CDG), Amsterdam Schiphol (AMS) and Frankfurt (FRA) with their strategic hub carriers, respectively, British Airways, Air France, KLM and Lufthansa, all compete for connecting traffic. Why? Connecting passengers are not necessarily big spenders in airport shops and restaurants but they account for 41% of the enplaned-deplaned passengers at these four airports.[7] In actual numbers, this is 100 million passengers, that's the population of Egypt, so while the yield may be low, the volume is high. On a broader scale, these extra 'bums in seats' make viable routes that would not otherwise be, so the airport punches above its weight, for example, daily service on an international route is now possible which then encourages local businesses to export more, international students to come and study and tourists to visit.

The additional belly cargo capacity stimulates exports because it reduces travel time, particularly important for perishable goods and puts downward pressure on freight rates.

As Figure 2.2 shows, the four traditional hubs have faced competition from secondary ones such as Copenhagen (CPH), Helsinki (HEL), Madrid (MAD), Munich (MUC) and Zurich (ZRH) which have increased their market share. However, to the extent that the major hubs are at capacity, some of this competition may be welcome as air carriers realign their networks to take advantage of quieter airports. For example, Lufthansa offloaded some demand from FRA to MUC and British Airways from LHR to London Gatwick (LGW). In other cases, smaller carriers such as Finnair decided there is a competitive advantage from building a niche Europe-Asia gateway at Helsinki (HEL).

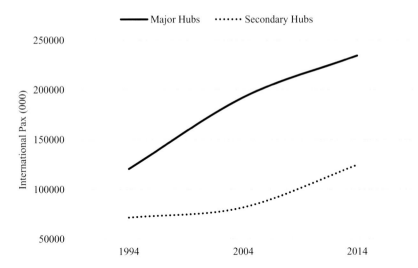

Figure 2.2 International Passenger Trends at Selected European Airports.
Source: Airports Council International (ACI) and various airport and government websites.

A similar situation exists on the West Coast of North America where Vancouver (YVR), Seattle-Tacoma (SEA), Portland (PDX), San Francisco (SFO) and Los Angeles (LAX) compete for connecting traffic between North America and Asia. Do any current competitors have plans to capture a greater share of the market? For example, SEA is building a new international arrivals facility which will greatly enhance the customer experience which today, because of congestion, often includes being held on the aircraft, after a 12-hour flight, until a gate with US Customs capacity is available. Meanwhile, YVR is constantly re-inventing the US to international connecting process to make it as competitive as a US airport. Even though travelling to Asia via YVR may be the fastest option, the impression of having to connect through a third country deters customers.

Turning to origin-destination passengers, airports can expand their catchment areas and see them contract too. Hong Kong International Airport (HKG) has over many years strategically increased the size of its ground catchment area by creating remote terminals with check-in, bag drop and pre-board screening at ports throughout the Pearl River Delta and connecting them to the airport by ferry.

Covering nine major cities in the PRD, SkyPier is now serving over 80 daily sailings taking passengers to destinations in Mainland China and Macau each day. In 2019, SkyPier reached to 2.19 million passengers, accounting for 3.1% of HKG passenger throughput.

Building on the success of this concept, HKG is developing the Intermodal Transfer Terminal (ITT) adjacent to the SkyPier and the corresponding bonded vehicular bridge linking up the Hong Kong Boundary Crossing Facilities of the new Hong Kong-Zhuhai-Macao Bridge (HZMB), scheduled for completion in 2022. This will make seamless bridge-to-air/air-to-bridge connections, so passengers arriving or departing HKG from Zhuhai and Macao via the HZMB will not have to clear immigration in Hong Kong.

NEW ENTRANTS

A new entrant can be an existing airport getting into a new line of business or a new, greenfield site. Probably the most significant debutantes in the last 25 years are from the Middle East, for example, Dubai (DXB), Abu Dhabi (AUH) and Doha (DOH). These are manifestations of an integrated national policy which harnesses the three components of a transportation system, the airports, the air carriers; Emirates, Etihad and Qatar, respectively, and the air navigation providers towards one objective: the growth and diversification of the economy. This is a classic case of hub building to stimulate tourism, investment, exports and education.

What is remarkable about Figure 2.3 is that Dubai (DXB) grew to be a larger airport than London Heathrow (LHR) in the space of 25 years. Yet, there is no evidence that DXB was the cause of LHR's

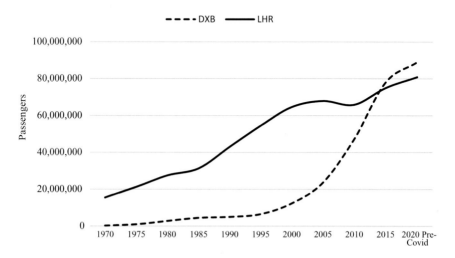

Figure 2.3 Incumbent and New Entrant Airports: Passenger Trends.

Source: Airports Council International (ACI) and airport and government websites.

slowdown; in fact, DXB has been mildly stimulative: a 10% growth in passenger volumes there has translated into a 0.5% increase in passengers at LHR, as Dubai has emerged as a destination in its own right and alternate connecting point to rapidly growing emerging markets like India and Africa.

Greater Sydney is a metropolitan area in New South Wales, Australia with a population of 5.3 million in 2019. It is Australia's most populous city, and Sydney Kingsford Smith Airport (SYD) is Australia's busiest passenger airport serving 44 million passengers in 2019. It is predominantly an origin-destination airport but an estimated 30% of passengers transfer between flights. It is the only commercial airport serving the Greater Sydney Region until Western Sydney Airport (WSA) opens which is currently scheduled to launch in 2026.

Sydney will then join the ranks of the world's metropolitan regions with multiple airports, which in Sydney's weight class would include San Francisco, Toronto and Chicago. The established model is that the primary airport serves over 95% of the international passenger traffic and between 70% and 80% of the domestic market. Domestic origin-destination demand with some 'sunspot' international charter flights is the niche that secondary airports occupy with all-cargo aircraft and business aviation as opportunities too. As shown in Table 2.1, there are formidable challenges facing WSA in prising an international carrier away from SYD.

Based on this model, WSA could be a 'cheap and cheerful' alternative to SYD particularly for domestic leisure travellers and the outer western suburbs of Sydney such as Parramatta and Blacktown where ground access to SYD is particularly challenging. The substitutes

Table 2.1 Western Sydney Airport Passenger Markets: Five Competitive Forces Summary

Western Sydney Airport Passenger Market: Competitive Assessment

Force	Comment	Threat Level
Bargaining power of customers	Only a few air carriers prepared to consider and commit to WSA.	High
Bargaining power of suppliers	Government agencies may be reluctant to split resources between SYD and WSA or SYD will lobby hard to retain them.	High
Existing competitors	SYD has critical mass, connecting passenger flows and a well-established ecosystem of fuel, catering, ground handling to support international operations.	High
New entrants	N/A	
Substitutes	Driving/Staycation/Lost Weekend.	Medium

for a trip to the Gold Coast, for example, would be driving there, vacationing at home or splurging on a 'lost weekend' in an upscale hotel. As we will see later in Chapter 5, WSA may have potential as an all-cargo airport.

Reinforcing this point is Figure 2.4 which shows how consumer interest in cheap flights in New South Wales is strongly and negatively correlated with domestic passenger volumes at SYD from which we can deduce that a lot of consumers are disappointed in the airfares available at SYD after controlling for seasonal variation and other factors. In other words, WSA could stimulate more air travel.

A good example of the complementarity that can develop between airports serving the same metropolitan area is the case of Toronto Pearson International Airport (YYZ) and Billy Bishop Toronto City Airport (YTZ). In 2018, YYZ served 49.5 million passengers and YTZ served 2.8 million. The latter is located about 5 km from Toronto CBD and used by turboprop aircraft[8] on short-haul routes to Montreal, Ottawa and some major US cities. It is very much a city-centre, business airport. As Toronto has evolved from a North American manufacturing centre to a global services city, it's arguable whether Pearson had the capacity to accommodate the associated increase in the propensity for air travel.[9] Billy Bishop has been a relief valve and there's evidence that by absorbing some of the short-haul origin-destination demand, it has freed up capacity for Pearson to develop into a global hub,[10] so Toronto, with two airports, is better connected overall.

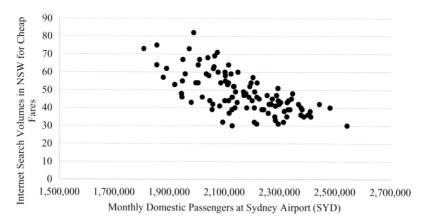

Figure 2.4 Western Sydney Airport: Consumer Interest in Low Fares.

Source: Author's calculations from Google Trends and Commonwealth Government BITRE data.

Undeniably there is a competitive element too. Passengers can fly from YTZ and connect to international destinations at Montreal (YUL) and Newark (EWR) and the two airports compete for scarce government resources such as border control.

SUBSTITUTES

In the pre-Covid 19 world, this fifth force was frequently glossed over, if not dismissed outright. Certainly, there are substitutes for short-haul trips, for example, high-speed rail in Europe has reduced the number of people flying between, for example, Amsterdam and Paris or between Madrid and Sevilla. The actual experience has been more nuanced. In China, HSR is a substitute for air on routes up to 1,000 km but it actually stimulated more air travel on city pairs over 1,000 km apart.[11] By bringing regions closer together, the pie got bigger for everyone. Finally, if HSR served the primary airport in the region, it gave that airport an advantage over secondary airports. As we will see in the next chapter, this is arguably one reason Amsterdam Schiphol (AMS) saw an uptick in its origin-destination passenger growth rate in 2010.

This recalls the old story of the buggy-whip manufacturers when the automobile became the dominant mode of personal transportation. They failed to comprehend that they were actually in the 'personal transportation accessory' business. Airports may have to conceive themselves more broadly too, for example, is there any reason why an airport should not invest in high-speed rail if it expands the catchment area and defers the need for a new runway?

We will likely see more substitution of short-haul flying by rail in the future for three reasons. First, as economies decarbonize, moving short-haul demand to rail that's powered by sustainable electricity is attractive relative to kerosene fuelled flights. Second, small aircraft flying short distances are probably not the highest and best use of hub airports' scarce runway capacity. Finally, congestion at hub airports often means air carriers' cancelling short-haul flights and unreliable service to regional airports. This can impair the local economy, for example, Diamond Aviation in London, Ontario, Canada cited difficulties like this in selling their corporate jets worldwide. London, Ontario is 90 km by air from Toronto Pearson and flights are frequently cancelled due to weather, congestion or air carriers' irregular operations leaving Diamond's sales force or visiting customers scrambling to make their connecting flights.

Competition from virtual meetings was not given much consideration before Covid-19 but now platforms like Zoom, WebEx and MS

Teams are very real substitutes for air travel. It is reasonable to assume that the quality of virtual meetings will continue to improve and equally reasonable to believe that while air travel will return to something approaching pre-pandemic normalcy, there will no doubt be additional processes to screen travellers health and vaccination status while the risks of borders shutting suddenly to contain flare-ups of Covid-19 or another virus are real and material. So, while everybody would probably agree that an in-person business or family gathering is preferable, a virtual meeting may be 'good enough' and in this respect, it is a classic disruptor.

AIRPORT BUSINESS SUB-COMPONENTS

Applying Porter's Five Forces at the airport macro-level is not without its challenges, for example, it's comparatively rare that a completely new airport will be built or that competitors will radically change business models. Most airports do a little bit of everything and air travel has been growing so fast that there has been plenty of business to go around. In fact, notional competitors are actually often complimentary. However, post-Covid, competition will probably become more intense.

The implicit assumption in the foregoing is that airports want volume growth and organically and not by mergers and acquisitions. However, yield growth is also a perfectly legitimate strategic objective and arguably a rational one if volume is choked off by finite capacity that, as discussed in Chapter 1, is difficult and expensive to increase but that is the subject for another book.

Porter's Five Forces framework can be helpful at the sub-component level of the business too. We focus on parking and duty free because real revenue per passenger from these businesses has been declining over recent years.

CAR PARKING

The competitive forces arrayed against an airport's car parking business are summarized in Table 2.2. It is a retail business in an established industry, so there are plenty of individual customers and suppliers of the necessary inputs: asphalt, paint, shuttle buses, software, etc.

For off-airport parking lots, they are known quantities, desire access to the curb and their products and services can easily be monitored.

Table 2.2 Car Parking: Five Competitive Forces Summary

Car Parking: Competitive Assessment

Force	Comment	Threat Level
Bargaining power of customers	Many customers.	Low
Bargaining power of suppliers	Many suppliers of parking equipment, software and management services.	Low
Existing competitors	Off-airport parking lots but value propositions can be adjusted accordingly.	Low
New entrants	Sharing Economy companies like Turo, Parking Panada. TNCs* such as Uber and Lyft. Airport rail access.	Medium
Substitutes	Declining rates of car ownership. Change in social and cultural habits around well-wishing and greeting at airports, intensified by pandemic.	High

Note: *Transportation Network Companies.

In any event, parking will not be the highest and best use as land values around airports increase.

The main competitive threats are new entrants and substitutes, for example, Turo is a peer-to-peer car-sharing platform that allows everyday car owners to rent out their car while they are not using it. Owners post the details of the car, its availability and price online. 'Guests' search for the car they need and book it through the online platform. Both the owner and the guest agree to set pick up and drop off times for the car, with the guest simply having to replace the gas they used. Imagine if the cars parked in the airport's lots are actually a shadow pool of car rental vehicles.

Parking Panda is an online service that allows a parking stall that would be otherwise empty to be rented out, for example, at home during work hours and on evenings and weekends at workplaces. The potential disruption to airports' car parking revenues is substantial as stalls at warehouses and offices in the vicinity of airports could be pressed into service to generate additional revenue for landlords. Figure 2.5 shows the rise in interest in this service.

New forms of ground access such as airport rail links or ride-sharing services like Uber and Lyft could be classified as new entrants but they are not necessarily a threat to parking revenues. The evidence suggests that parking rates can be increased when an alternative, affordable form of ground access becomes available and while it's early days, services such as Uber and Lyft appear to compete with public transit more than with car parking.

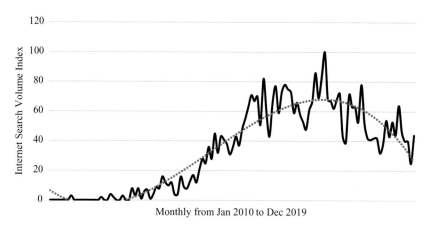

Figure 2.5 Consumer Interest in Alternative Airport Parking Providers.
Source: Google Trends.

A mobile phone now gives precise arrival times of aircraft which enables lurking on obscure roadways and driveways waiting for the call from the passenger that they're ready to be picked up.

Turning to substitutes, we are seeing a long-term decline in vehicle ownership rates as Figure 2.6 illustrates but there are other social and cultural changes in the propensity for passengers to be met or sent off

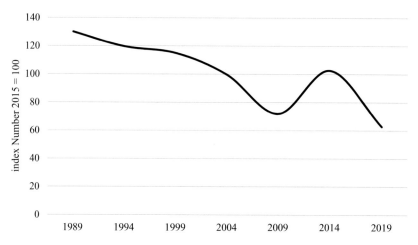

Figure 2.6 Changing Propensity for Car Ownership.
Source: OECD, passenger car registrations in the US retrieved from FRED, Federal Reserve Bank of St. Louis.

at airports, which affects the demand for short-term parking, often the most lucrative and, of course, the pandemic may accelerate these trends.

DUTY FREE

Looking now at duty free, the main threats again are from new entrants and substitutes, as summarized in Table 2.3.

In terms of existing competitors, to the extent that passenger crew interaction is curtailed in a post-Covid world, in-flight duty free is probably going to remain a small player not to mention that additional fuel required to carry a reasonable inventory of products. It remains to be seen how arrivals duty free will slot in with Covid tests on arrival, social distancing and transfer to mandatory quarantine facilities.

As far as new entrants are concerned, it is notable that Alibaba, the Chinese online shopping giant, has acquired 10% of world duty free operator, Dufry. It plans to offer luxury goods at lower tax rates in China even though residents are not travelling internationally. Skybuys has an app rolled out at SYD, letting passengers buy duty free online before they fly, at the airport or mid-flight and collect it when exiting the airport. These new channels may increase the overall size of the duty-free market but airports will have to recalibrate business models and contracts to continue the flow of concession revenues. However, this will be from a weaker bargaining position to the extent that airport, as the physical place where the transaction occurs, is no longer central to the business. Another factor pushing sales online will be maintaining social distancing in shops, post-pandemic. Substitutes for duty free include changing patterns of alcohol and tobacco consumption and consumer preferences for luxury goods. Will the social status signalled by a memorable Instagram photo become more valuable than a Prada bag?

Table 2.3 Duty Free: Five Competitive Forces Summary

Duty Free: Competitive Assessment

Force	Comment.	Threat Level
Bargaining power of customers	Many customers.	Low
Bargaining power of suppliers	Limited number of global operators. Government liquor monopolies.	Medium
Existing competitors	In-flight duty-free, arrivals duty-free, duty-paid stores.	Medium
New entrants	Alibaba/Skybuys.	High
Substitutes	Changing propensities for luxury purchases, alcohol and tobacco consumption.	Medium

Arguably, a sixth competitive force is government policy and regulation. An editorial in the *Economist*[12] magazine recently argued that duty-free shopping is essentially a tax break for the rich should be phased out.

SUMMARY AND CONCLUSIONS

'Fast, cheap and good: pick two'. Many airports try to be all things to all people which leads to strategic bluntness which can be costly. The example of Austin Airport (AUS) trying to wrangle a low-cost terminal into a full-service corporate culture is illustrative.

A clear strategy, meaning one that correctly diagnoses the problem and sets out a way to deal with it, free of noble words, is necessary to maximize returns and retain social licence without which the wheels may spin but forward momentum will be elusive. In the past, the rapid growth of the air travel pie has forgiven a lot of strategic bluntness but that is no longer the case.

The kind of competition airports were experiencing was already changing before the pandemic particularly from new entrants and substitutes which by their nature are more difficult to discern and respond to than the traditional competitors.

Then Covid-19 came along and, in the post-pandemic era, airports will have to adapt to the fundamental changes in how we work, communicate and travel that Covid has wrought. In other words, the importance of having a clear strategy has never been greater.

NOTES

1. Rumelt, Good Strategy/Bad Strategy.
2. IATA, "Level of Service".
3. aka "Awesome" and "Execrable".
4. Ashford, "Level of Service Design", 5–21.
5. Not all low-cost airlines owned by airlines are doomed to failure, for example, Qantas and JetStar. Separation is partly maintained by the former being headquartered in Sydney and the latter in Melbourne.
6. Airports will have as many catchment areas as they have markets. For example, the catchment area for domestic business travel will be small because of these passengers' high value of time while the catchment areas of international leisure travel, where time is less pressing and fares could be considerably cheaper at a more distant airport, will be much larger.

7. Author's estimates based on data from Airports Council International and from the individual airports.
8. Jet aircraft are not allowed to use YTZ for noise reasons.
9. In 2001, Toronto CMA generated 4.1 origin-destination trips (at both airports) per capita and by 2016 that had increased by 37% to 5.6 trips per capita.
10. Each air carrier movement at YTZ results in 24 more connecting passengers at YYZ so if Air Canada can divert 24 passengers travelling from Toronto to Montreal from YYZ to YTZ, it has 24 seats to sell to passengers travelling, for example, from Tokyo-Montreal via YYZ.
11. Zhang, Graham, and Wong, "Quantifying the Substitutability", 191–215.
12. February 27, 2021.

. . . .

BIBLIOGRAPHY

Ashford, Norman. "Level of Service Design Concept for Airport Passenger Terminals – A European View". *Transportation Planning and Technology* 12, no. 1 (1988): 5–21. https://doi.org/10.1080/03081068808717356.

IATA. "Level of Service Concept". Accessed January 18, 2021. https://www.iata.org/en/services/consulting/airport-pax-security/level-of-service/.

Rumelt, Richard. *Good Strategy/Bad Strategy*. New York, NY, Crown Publishing Group, 2011.

Zhang, Fangni, Daniel J. Graham, and Mark Siu Chun Wong. "Quantifying the Substitutability and Complementarity between High-Speed Rail and Air Transport". *Transportation Research Part A: Policy and Practice* 118 (December 2018): 191–215. https://doi.org/10.1016/j.tra.2018.08.004.

3 DEMAND FORECASTING

The famous Canadian economist, John Kenneth Galbraith, once said that the purpose of economic forecasting was to make astrology look good. In a similar vein, economists have predicted five out of the last three recessions. All joking aside, planning means forecasting how many people, packages and planes will land at an airport at some point in the future.

THE S-CURVE

Change is rarely linear. More often, it resembles an S-curve. Illustrated in Figure 3.1 this is a well-established concept in business and technology with the basic point being that the demand for a product or the adoption of a new technology over time tends to follow the same pattern: growth is slow at the outset, then accelerates and slows again. In the first stage, the product enters the market, a few early adopters buy it, then growth accelerates as it becomes a mass market product until demand is saturated and growth tails off levels. The transitions from slow to fast to slow growth again are referred to as inflection points. Obviously, many products do not make it to mass market stage and the length of the stages can be one year, ten years or even one hundred years.

Bill Gates is quoted as saying that people overestimate the change that will occur in three years but underestimate the change in ten years. This captures the essence of the S-curve: slow adoption of a new product, so in three years you do not see a lot of difference but ten years later, everybody has one.

A classic example is the uptake of mobile phone use in the US. As Figure 3.2 shows, in 1980, nobody had a mobile phone but by 1990, a few adventurous individuals were carrying 'bricks'. Fast forward and today quizzical looks are cast at people using a payphone on the street, assuming they can find one in working order.

  DOI: 10.4324/9781003173267-3

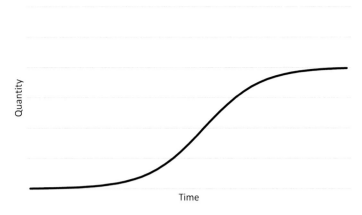

Figure 3.1 Generic S-curve.

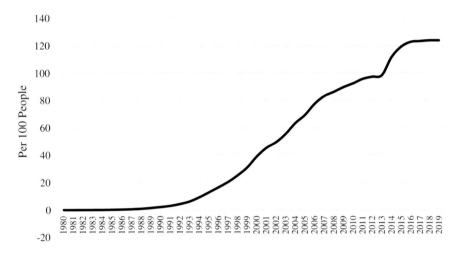

Figure 3.2 S-curve: Mobile Phone Use.

Source: World Bank, Mobile Cellular Subscriptions in the US, retrieved from FRED, Federal Reserve Bank of St. Louis; https://fred.stlouisfed.org/series/.

To use an example from aviation, Figure 3.3 shows the percentage of households in Vancouver, Canada reporting the purchase of an airline ticket over the last 70 years. Air travel was very much a novelty in the 1950s and 1960s with only 5%–10% of households so reporting. From the 1970s to the 1990s, air travel entered the mainstream with 35%–40% of households taking a trip by air after which market maturity was reached.

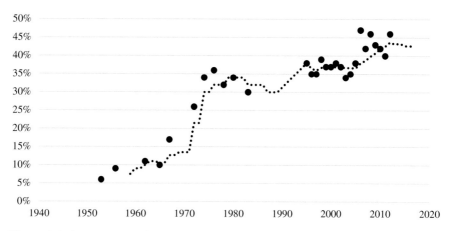

Figure 3.3 S-curve: Household Spending on Airline Tickets.
Source: Statistics Canada: Surveys of Household Spending.

In terms of the strategic trilemma we talked about in Chapter 2, the first phase is often the fast and cheap one as the product has some imperfections but is priced attractively to get a toe-hold in the market. The second, mass market phase is characterized by cheap and good since economies of scale drive production costs down and to be successful the product must be good. In the final phase, the product has been incrementally improved but to protect margins, it's no longer the price leader. Of course this is the inflection point at which disruptors enter the market offering a product that's good enough but at a lower price point.

If we look at the growth trajectory of traffic at most airports over a long period of time, we see an S-curve. The key task in airport planning is knowing where you are on that curve and the timing, direction and magnitude of the next inflection point. In the case studies that follow, we look back over 50 years in some cases and by looking at traffic changes over a five-year interval to remove some of the noise from the trendline and focus on the 'signal'.

CASE STUDY: TORONTO PEARSON INTERNATIONAL AIRPORT

The trajectory of growth in passengers at Toronto Pearson International Airport, Canada is shown in Figure 3.4. From 1965 to 1980, the demand for air travel steadily increases until 1980 when the first inflection point

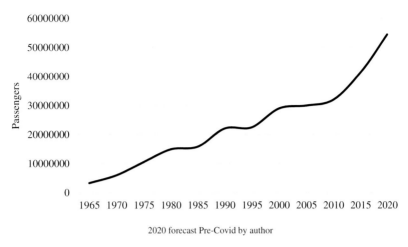

2020 forecast Pre-Covid by author

Figure 3.4 S-curves: Toronto Pearson International Airport 2020 Forecast Pre-Covid by Author.

Source: Greater Toronto Airports Authority, Transport Canada.

is hit. From 1980 to 1985, growth is flat as Canada suffers a severe recession, oil prices and therefore airfares increase. However, in 1984, the Government of Canada substantially deregulated the domestic aviation market, so there's an inflection point in 1985 after which growth resumes. In the case of Toronto Pearson one of the consequences of deregulation was the creation of a hub and spoke network by air carriers so YYZ benefited more than most. Another inflection point occurred in 1990 with the Gulf War and an economic downturn which flattened demand. Another major policy change took place in 1995 when the US and Canada signed an Open Skies agreement which stimulated transborder demand. From 2000 to 2010, passenger traffic at Toronto Pearson barely grew for a variety of reasons: the bursting of the 'Dotcom bubble' in 2000, the 9/11 terrorist attacks, SARS, the bankruptcy of Air Canada, the leakage of Canadian travellers to US border airports and the Great Financial Crisis (GFC) in 2009. Finally, the last inflection point occurred in 2010 which ushered in a ten-year period, before Covid-19, of rapid growth due to the convergence of several factors. These include the declining real cost of air travel, Toronto's evolution from a manufacturing to service-based economy, Canada's two major carriers building hubs at Pearson and economic prosperity.

The strategic foresight would have been to see, in the depths of the recession in 2009, that the following year would be the beginning of a decade of continuous, rapid growth.

Case Study: Seattle-Tacoma International Airport

Another example is Seattle-Tacoma International Airport (SEA) in the US. Figure 3.5 shows that slow but steady growth characterized the years from 1990 to 2000 but in the next ten years, SEA was flat only adding 2.2 million passengers. Traffic was adversely impacted by the 9/11 terrorist attacks in 2001, hitting the busy short-haul services to Portland, Oregon (PDX) particularly hard and then the Great Financial Crisis in 2009. Then, in 2010, SEA hit another inflection point and growth took off driven by a strong local economy but more specifically Delta Airlines selecting SEA as its Asia-Pacific gateway. Delta's share of total passengers jumped from 6% in 2009 to 24% in 2019. It would have been courageous then for the planners at the Port of Seattle to predict what actually happened in the second decade of the new century.

Case Study: Cincinnati

If SEA is a good example of what happens when an air carrier decides to build a strategic hub, Cincinnati-Northern Kentucky International Airport (CVG) shows what happens when a carrier dismantles one. At its

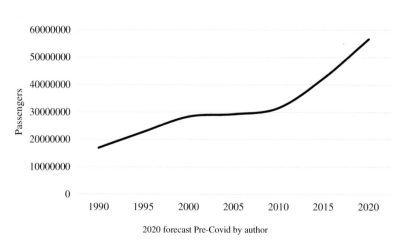

2020 forecast Pre-Covid by author

Figure 3.5 S-curves: Seattle-Tacoma International Airport 2020 Forecast Pre-Covid by Author.

Source: Port of Seattle.

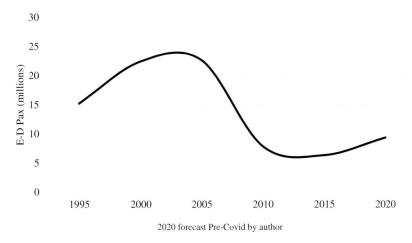

Figure 3.6 S-curves: Cincinnati-Northern Kentucky International Airport 2020 Forecast Pre-Covid by Author.

Source: Cincinnati-Northern Kentucky International Airport.

zenith in 2005, CVG was one of the biggest single air carrier hubs in the world and as a community, Cincinnati was extraordinarily well connected to the world helping sustain it as the headquarters for Fortune 500 companies like Proctor and Gamble. However, Delta filed for bankruptcy in September 2005, merged with Northwest Airlines in 2008 and the subsequent rationalization of networks resulted in CVG reverting to a spoke. By 2015, CVG was serving 16 million, that is, 72%, fewer passengers than it was ten years earlier, as illustrated in Figure 3.6.

CASE STUDY: HONOLULU INTERNATIONAL AIRPORT

In the case of Honolulu International Airport (HNL), we see two inflection points due to changes in aircraft technology and air navigation rules, as illustrated in Figure 3.7. The first is the advent of the jet age in the 1960s which put Hawaii within five hours flying time of the west coast of North America and eight hours of Japan, ushering in the era of mass tourism. Traffic grew steadily and peaked at HNL in the mid-1990s but then declined by 26% over the next 15 years. It was not for want of local demand as over the same period, Hawaii's resident population increased by 16% and total visitor arrivals by air increased by 7%.

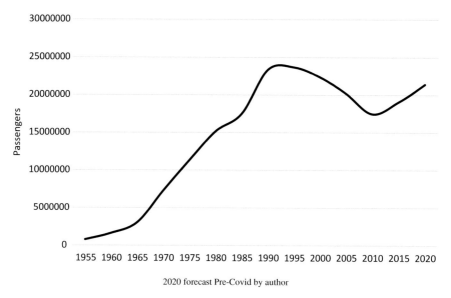

2020 forecast Pre-Covid by author

Figure 3.7 S-curves: Honolulu International Airport 2020 Forecast Pre-Covid by Author.

Source: US FAA, Hawaii Dept of Transportation.

So, what happened? ETOPS[1] happened. Before 1985, twin-engine aircraft could only fly a route that took them no more than 60 minutes away from a suitable airport, in case one engine failed. In 1985, based on advances in jet engine technology, the FAA modified this rule to 120 minutes and in 1988 extended it to 180 minutes. ETOPS imposes rigorous maintenance and operation standards that allow two-engine aircraft to fly across large bodies of water like the Pacific Ocean. The effect of this was to make long, thin trans-Pacific routes commercially viable. Arguably, ETOPS has been a mixed blessing for HNL. On the one hand, it allows B737 aircraft to fly from smaller markets on the West Coast of North America but, on the other hand, some aircraft and passengers that previously had to stop in HNL to refuel or connect, no longer had to do so. ETOPS also made routes from the West Coast hubs to the smaller Hawaiian Islands such as Maui and Kauai viable. As a result, HNL's share of air arrivals in Hawaii declined from 74% in 1995 to 62% in 2010.

The recovery in traffic since 2010 is due to favourable economic conditions, Hawaiian Airlines building a mid-Pacific hub and the advent of Airbnb which removes the constraints of finite hotel room capacity imposed on the number of visitors.

CASE STUDY: HONG KONG INTERNATIONAL AIRPORT

Undeniably, Hong Kong International Airport's S-curves (HKG) are less 'curvy', befitting a mega hub airport serving a rapidly growing region. It has the critical mass to absorb shocks more easily. Looking back at passenger traffic over the last 50 years, we see growth accelerating between 1985 and 1995 after which it slowed again, despite the opening of the new airport at Chek Lap Kok in 1998 but which coincided with a financial crisis in Asia when Hong Kong's economy shrink by 7.2% over two years. SARS depressed growth in the 2000–2005 period with a 20% decline in passengers in 2003 alone. Growth resumed and accelerated, partly due to HKG's strategy of bringing the Pearl River Delta into its ground catchment area, through to 2019 when civil unrest deterred visitors and damaged the economy. Figure 3.8 illustrates these patterns.

CASE STUDY: BUFFALO, NY

So far, we have looked at mainly large airports. Do smaller ones exhibit S-curves too? Yes, as Figure 3.9 shows for Buffalo-Niagara Falls International Airport, New York (BUF). Serving a metropolitan

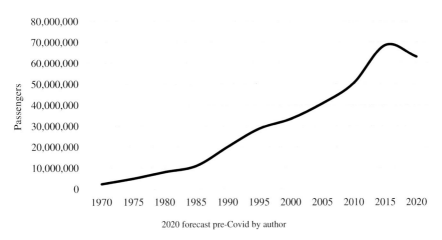

2020 forecast pre-Covid by author

Figure 3.8 S-curves: Hong Kong International Airport 2020 Forecast Pre-Covid by Author.

Source: Hong Kong CAA.

area of just under 1 million people in north-west corner of the state on the US-Canada border, its catchment area includes Toronto, Ontario, Canada with a metropolitan population of 6 million less than two hours' drive away. The airport served about 2.5 million passengers in 2019. For various reasons including a larger, denser and more competitive market, US airfares are lower per mile than Canadian ones and when the Canadian dollar appreciates in value, it makes flying from a US airport, close to the border, more attractive for Canadians. Notably, BUF had its busiest three years when the Canadian and US dollars were at parity, in fact, every 10% stronger the Canadian dollar is, passenger volumes at BUF go up by 3.2%. In 2009, when the Canadian dollar was at parity, and just before the last inflection point in Figure 3.9, 38% of the passengers at BUF were Canadians.[2] The main drivers of passenger growth at BUF are not local economic conditions but the exchange rate and the state of the Canadian economy. This means is that sometimes you must look beyond your boundaries to see the next inflection point.

Another way of illustrating this is by looking at Internet search patterns. Figure 3.10 shows Internet search volumes in Ontario, Canada of the term 'cheap flights from Buffalo' (the dotted line) and the Canada/US exchange rate (the solid line). As it becomes less expensive for Canadians to buy US dollars, the low point on the solid line, their interest in flying from Buffalo Airport (the dotted line) increases.

The time of maximum hazard for any product is when the growth rate slows at the top of the S-curve. The rapid growth period is over and

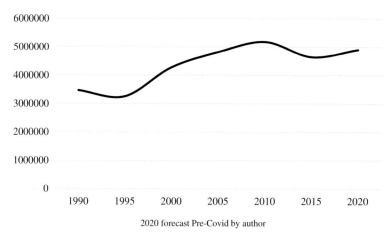

2020 forecast Pre-Covid by author

Figure 3.9 S-curves: Buffalo-Niagara Falls International Airport 2020 Forecast Pre-Covid by Author.

Source: US Bureau of Transportation Statistics, FAA, Wikipedia.

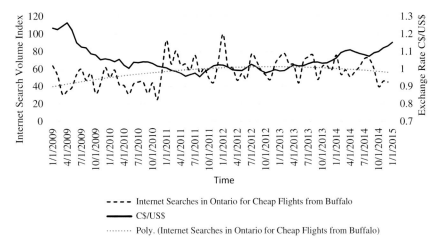

Figure 3.10 Canadian Consumer Interest in Cheap Flights.
Source: Google Trends, Board of Governors of the Federal Reserve System (US), Canada/U.S. Foreign Exchange Rate retrieved from FRED, Federal Reserve Bank of St. Louis.

an uncertain future beckons. In some cases, the product's intrinsic value, indeed its very familiarity, can usher in a long period of slow growth. If the brand is strong incremental improvements can sustain it for a long time. The other outcomes are that demand falls as new products come into the market. These may be disruptors, as we discussed in Chapter 2, that offer a product that's not as good as the incumbent but 'good enough'. A good example of this is Vancouver households' spending on airline tickets. If you look at Figure 3.3 carefully, there is another inflection point starting in about 2005 when the share of households buying airline tickets kicks up to the 40% range. This is of strategic importance since it reflects the tendency of Canadians to use airports just across the US border where fares, certainly to US destinations, are often much cheaper. In other words, even though they entailed a longer drive in many cases and had fewer amenities, US border airports were 'good enough' for a lot of Canadians.

FORECASTING TECHNIQUES

Master Plans have a chapter on forecasts which will invariably contain a graph with three straight lines heading upward over time, showing the low, base-case and high forecast of traffic growth. It's almost as if the inflection generating changes in aircraft technology (long-range, twin-engine jets), air navigation practices (ETOPS), government policy changes (deregulation), air carrier strategy (hub building and hub dismantling) and exchange rates have been banished. Of course, these are all external inflections but what if the airport is successfully executing its strategy? By definition, this will create an inflection, for example, a secondary airport may lure a low-cost carrier or adopt 'small is beautiful' branding to differentiate itself from the large hub.

The straight lines are a product of the most common forecasting approach which is an economic one that uses regression analysis to predict the demand for air travel based on the size of the economy as measured by Gross Domestic Product (GDP).[3] Other factors considered include the structure of the economy as well as air fares and household income.

Historical data on GDP are widely available and for long periods of time and it is a standard economic forecast. We always use real GDP, that is, with inflation stripped out, so we capture the underlying growth rate of the economy, not just increase in general price levels for the same basket of goods and services.

The beauty of regression analysis allows us to isolate the impacts of an individual variable, amongst many. For example, we may find that a 1% change in the size of the economy produces a 1.2% increase in the demand for air travel but a 1% increase in oil prices, which feeds through into air fares, depresses demand by 0.5%. We can then model various scenarios of economic growth and oil prices. These two variables are connected but regression analysis controls for that too. When you read or hear an expression like 'all other things equal' or 'controlling for other factors', this is a sure-fire sign that regression analysis has been employed.

Regression analysis also allows us to see lagged effects, for example, a change in the demand for air travel in response to a variable may not occur immediately.

When we think about the structure of the economy and how it affects the demand for air travel, we are really looking at two things: services and exports. For example, the services sector has a higher propensity for air travel than manufacturing because there is more human interaction. The service sector's share of employment in Ontario, Canada grew from 65% in 1981 to 81% in 2019. When we correlate this with growth at Toronto Pearson International Airport, this structural change had a small but significant, lagged impact.

The greater the export orientation of an economy, the more international travel will take place. An export occurs when a non-resident buys something produced in a country. It could be a tangible item such as piece of clothing, seafood or an engine part but it can also be a service, for example, tourism or international education. The tuition fees that a student from the People's Republic of China pays to Imperial College, London, for example, gets counted as a service export in the UK's national accounts.

As domestic businesses seek international markets, travel occurs to meet potential customers, build relationships, provide after sales support or iron out logistics and regulatory problems. Looking back over almost 40 years' worth data at Pearson, we see that the share of Ontario's economy accounted for by international exports has a small but significant effect on international passenger volumes.

It would be reasonable to say that this is a necessary but not sufficient step in forecasting. So, start by generating an aggregate passenger traffic forecast based on a standard economic forecasting methodology on top of which are layered scenarios of potential inflection points. In other words, if you see a straight-line forecast, prod it.

While these are general rules, forecasters need to acknowledge the context of the propensity for air travel, development, the implications of airport size, the other components of the transportation system and regional airports.

PROPENSITY FOR AIR TRAVEL

We also need to be mindful of where a country sits on the economic development scale. If average incomes, measured in terms of GDP per capita, are in the $5,000–$15,000 range the underlying growth rate will be faster than in a higher income country with a mature air travel market. Why is this? Several reasons including a middle class emerging between these income bands with an appetite for air travel, closer integration into the global economy and an openness to tourism.

This relationship is clear in Figure 3.11 which shows how as countries become wealthier, the propensity for air travel increases. On the bottom axis is GDP per capita and the left axis is the number of airport passengers per capita in a country, a measure of the propensity for air travel.[4]

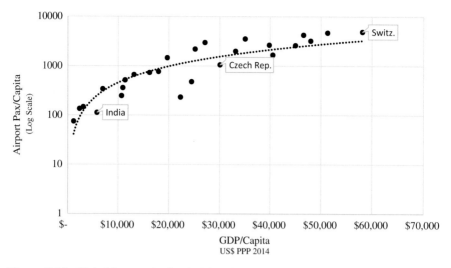

Figure 3.11 Global Propensity for Air Travel.

Source: compiled by author using GDP data from International Monetary Fund (IMF) and passenger data from Airports Council International (ACI).

CASE STUDY: BRAZIL AND MALAYSIA

Figure 3.12 shows two examples: Brazil and Malaysia. In both cases, we see classic S-curves and inflection points between $5,000 and $15,000 GDP per capita when the demand[5] for air travel, shown by the dashed line, takes off.

SYSTEM FORECASTING

FUNCTIONALLY

An interesting exercise would be to compare the forecasts of the air navigation provider, air carriers and airports to get a sense of what assumptions underlay them. Obviously, each operates on different timelines and is more or less public about its forecasts but on a percentage basis how many units does the air navigation company anticipate flying through its airspace and how many aircraft seats do the air carriers have on order? The results can be revealing; it's almost a form of self-criticism.

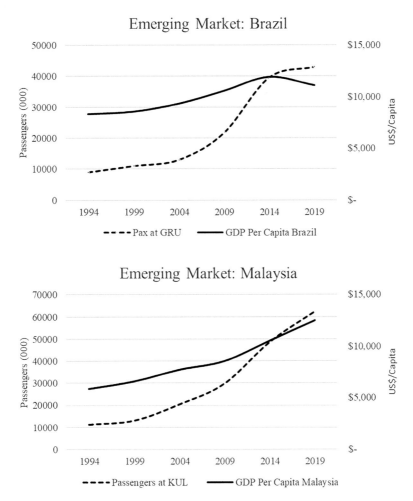

Figure 3.12 Brazil and Malaysia: Propensity for Air Travel.

Source: Airports Council International, Wikipedia and University of Groningen and University of California, Davis, Real GDP at Constant National Prices for Brazil and Malaysia, retrieved from FRED, Federal Reserve Bank of St. Louis.

GEOGRAPHICALLY

Consistent with the theme of beyond the boundaries, if we accept that airports compete and complement each other in a system, we need to forecast regional demand first and then allocate to airports based on the competitive strengths and weaknesses.

This drives at the question as to the latent demand for air travel and how is it distributed amongst other airports.

It would be reasonable to say that this is a necessary but not sufficient step in forecasting. So, a first step would be an aggregate passenger traffic forecast based on a standard economic forecasting methodology on top of which are layered scenarios of potential inflection points. In other words, if you see a straight-line forecast, take a step back and consider what the next inflection point could be.

As a measure for the propensity for air travel to and from a metropolitan area, we are going to use origin-destination passengers per capita. What would cause this number to be higher or lower? An airport with an affluent catchment area, with a service-oriented economy, in a tourist region with no competing airports nearby would tend to have a higher rate of origin-destination passengers per capita or one that is attracting passengers from another region.

Figure 3.13 shows this for selected Canadian metropolitan areas in 2017. Kelowna, BC (YLW) has the highest rate reflecting its affluent catchment area, year-round tourist appeal and long drive to the next airport of a reasonable size.[6]

By contrast, the metros with the lowest rates are Hamilton, Ontario (YHM) and London, Ontario (YXU), which leak business to Toronto Pearson (YYZ) and US border airports like Buffalo (BUF) and Detroit (DTW). Nor are Hamilton and London, Ontario noted tourist

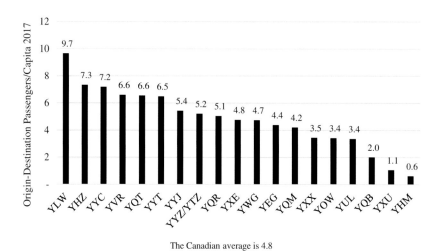

The Canadian average is 4.8

Figure 3.13 Selected Canadian Metropolitan Area: Propensity for Air Travel the Canadian Average is 4.8.

Source: Various Airports and Statistics Canada.

destinations. Likewise, Quebec City (YQB) is within the gravitational pull of Montreal, Quebec (YUL) and while Quebec City is very much a visitor attraction and services-based economy but there's a low resident propensity for air travel.

The point being is that if an airport has a low origin-destination per passenger rate, is it because the catchment area has a latent low propensity for air travel either because of income levels, the structure of the economy, being off the tourist trail or leakage to another airport?

AIRPORT SIZE

Simply put, larger airports have critical mass, meaning they are more resilient. A smaller airport serving an economy dependent on one industry is more exposed to fluctuations while the larger one serves many markets, so a recession in one region can be offset by growth elsewhere. Also, when air carriers rationalize their networks in downturns, smaller airports are more vulnerable. To illustrate this point, global hub airports generally suffered a smaller decline in traffic during the GFC[7] than smaller airports, for example, Figure 3.14 shows the changes in the UK economy (columns) compared to passenger volumes, shown by solid and dashed lines respectively, at two of the UK's biggest airports, London Heathrow (LHR) and Manchester (MAN). The UK economy contracted by 7.3%

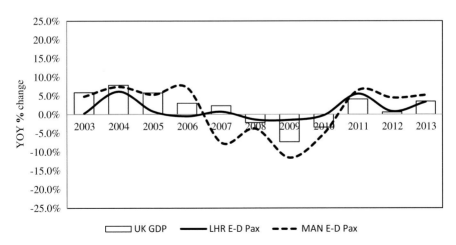

Figure 3.14 Airport Size and Resilience.
Source: Heathrow and Manchester Airports, IMF.

in 2009 but LHR's traffic only fell by 1.5%. Manchester Airport, which is a secondary hub with a smaller, less diversified market experienced a 11.6% decline.

FORECAST OUTPUTS

ORIGIN-DESTINATION VS CONNECTING PASSENGERS

For more insight, let's look at a major European hub, Amsterdam Schiphol Airport (AMS) and break down total enplaned-deplaned passengers into its two constituent parts: origin-destination and connecting. The distinction is important for planning purposes because connecting passengers do not use ground transportation, car parking or check-in or bag claim facilities.

Remember that one enplaned-deplaned passenger is one pair of feet getting on or off a plane. Those feet could be starting or ending their journey at AMS or just changing planes. One round trip connecting itinerary via AMS therefore translates into four enplaned-deplaned passengers which is why dehubbing has such a calamitous impact on traffic. As Figure 3.15 shows, over a 25-year period, we see a familiar S-curve pattern with an inflection point after 2009 after which passenger

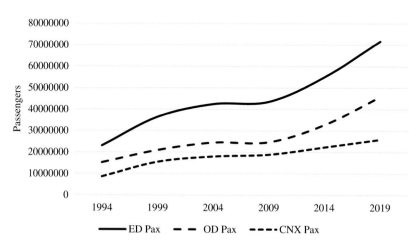

Figure 3.15 S-curves: Amsterdam Schiphol Airport.
Source: Schiphol Airport.

volumes grow faster but only in the origin-destination market. In fact, the connecting ratio fell from 42% in 2010 to 36% in 2019 which is a material reduction in ten years for a major hub airport. One reason for the inflection may be the commencement of high-speed rail service to Schiphol in 2009 increasing the ground catchment area of AMS. The growth in origin-destination volumes had some challenges too such as the Dutch government in July 2018 introducing a tax on all passengers originating at AMS which drove, literally, some of this market to neighbouring airports in Belgium and Germany. The tax was rescinded one year later.

At an annual level, if we look at Amsterdam Schiphol Airport (AMS), we see a very strong correlation (0.96) between enplaned-deplaned passenger volumes and the Netherlands economy. Building a forecast model off that relationship, as illustrated in Figure 3.16, we get a forecast that is within 1.6% of actual passengers, on average, over the almost 25-year forecast period. The key relationship is that a 1% increase in the size of the Netherlands economy results in a 1.4% increase in enplaned-deplaned passengers at AMS. A very simple forecast for AMS would be taking the predictions for the growth of the Netherlands economy and multiplying them by 1.4 to convert them into anticipated passenger growth at AMS.

The forecast did not fully capture the downturn during Global Financial Crisis of 2008–2010 because air travel is a discretionary item, gets cut first by both businesses and households so airport traffic will

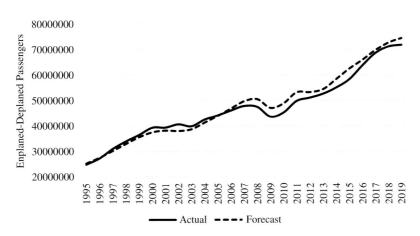

Figure 3.16 Amsterdam Schiphol Airport: Actual and Forecast Enplaned-Deplaned Passengers.

Source: Actual data from Schiphol Airport, forecast by author.

decline disproportionately. The model is reasonably good at tracking the trajectory of growth after 2010, from a slightly higher base, but the divergence widens in 2018 and 2019.

As forecasts get more granular, we usually see the forecast to actual variance increase. In this case, the average variation to actual is 2.2% compared to 1.6% for enplaned-deplaned passengers. The divergence is greater during the Great Financial Crisis (GFC) because the origin-destination market is more closely tied to the fate of the Netherlands economy, for example, from 2008 to 2009, origin-destination passengers decline by 8.9% on a GDP contraction of 3.7%, as shown in Figure 3.17.

Turning now to connecting passengers (Figure 3.18), we substitute the GDP of the European Union for the GDP of the Netherlands to reflect the role of AMS as a major European hub. This results in a better forecast with the variance averaging 0.2%. Because the EU market is large and more diverse, the amplitude of variations tends to be smaller, for example, from 2008 to 2009, connecting passengers declined by 7.2%, less than origin-destination passengers but on a larger reduction in GDP of 4.3%.

Most airports collect connecting data based on air carriers' filings which tends to only capture passengers changing planes on the same carrier or alliance. The Internet had made it easier for passengers to build their own connecting itineraries on two unrelated airlines but which

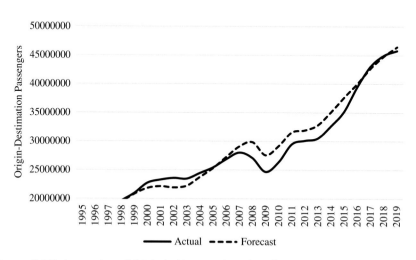

Figure 3.17 Amsterdam Schiphol Airport: Actual and Forecast Origin-Destination Passengers.

Source: Actual data from Schiphol Airport, forecast by author.

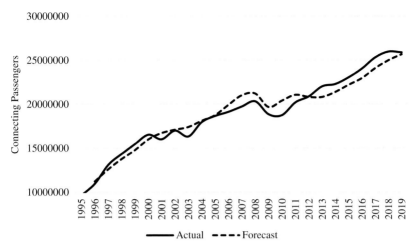

Figure 3.18 Amsterdam Schiphol Airport: Actual and Forecast Connecting Passengers.
Source: Actual data from Schiphol Airport, forecast by author.

show up in the data as two origin-destination trips. The point is that connecting passenger volumes may be undercounted and under forecast.

DOMESTIC VS INTERNATIONAL

The most common practice is to forecast domestic and international passengers since at many airports, they use separate terminal buildings and put different demands on them. For example, international terminals are bigger due to the exigencies of border processes and the opportunity to sell duty-free while international passengers tend to be accompanied to and from the airport with a larger number of greeters and well-wishers.

Let's use Los Angeles International Airport (LAX) as a case study. The largest airport on the West Coast of the US, it has a mix of international and domestic passengers and, unlike SEA, is not dominated by a single carrier. In 2019, the air carrier with the largest market share was American Airlines at 19.4%. What is most interesting about the S-curves for LAX, shown in Figure 3.19, is that the larger, more mature domestic market has more pronounced inflection points than the international one.

A couple of things may explain this: competition at LAX between air carriers and between LAX and other domestic airports in the region such as Orange County (SNA), Burbank (BUR) and Ontario (ONT) makes it more dynamic. The growth in domestic traffic between 2009 and 2019 was because LAX increased its share of the market from 66% in 2010 to 71% in 2019 at the expense of those airports. This is quite a remarkable shift considering the size and maturity of this market. One explanation

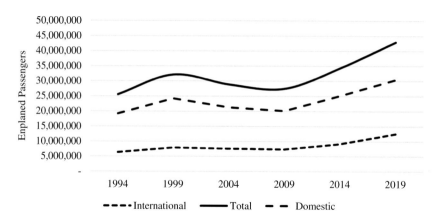

Figure 3.19 S-curves: LAX.
Source: Los Angeles World Airports.

is that predominantly domestic air carriers, such as Southwest Airlines, are increasingly attracted to international hub airports, which they formerly avoided. It gives them access to that market even though they do not belong to one of the global alliances and passengers are increasingly building DIY connections, that is, buying two separate origin-destination tickets and then self-connecting. Some evidence of this is provided by Internet search patterns. Figure 3.20 shows travel related Internet searches in the US for the following terms 'LAX Terminal Southwest'

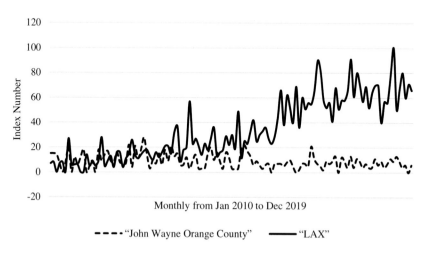

Figure 3.20 Consumer Interest in Southwest Airlines in Los Angeles.
Source: Google Trends.

and 'Southwest Orange County Airport'. As you can see in Figure 3.20, interest in Southwest Airlines at LAX has grown but is flat at SNA.

Bi-lateral air services agreements between the US and other countries limit frequency and capacity so the slow growth in international traffic may reflect that but also the ability of long-range aircraft coming from Asia to the US to by-pass the traditional West Coast gateways. For example, Qantas flies non-stop from Sydney (SYD) to Dallas-Fort Worth (DFW). The other reason may be a slow-down in global trade precipitated by the policies of President Trump.

The correlation between domestic and international passengers is very strong for the simple reason that they are in many cases the same people, that is, somebody getting off a plane from Tokyo and then boarding one to Phoenix, Arizona.

RESIDENT VS NON-RESIDENT

Another sub-forecast is to break origin-destination passengers down into residents and non-residents. This is comparatively rare but can help the planning of ground access infrastructure. Airports serving predominantly non-resident origin-destination passengers will typically have larger facilities for car rentals and tour buses, for example, Orlando, Florida or Malaga, Spain and less long-term car parking whereas it will be the other way round at Cleveland, Ohio and Hamburg, Germany.

FREQUENT VS INFREQUENT TRAVELLERS

This is very rare because it's not particularly relevant for facility planning, but nonetheless is of strategic value. Do you think that Amazon knows who its best customers are? Or Air France? Of course, they do and they spend a lot of time and money securing this loyalty. With a few exceptions, airports would be hard pressed to say the same. Of 20 million annual enplaned-deplaned passengers which, remember, are just pairs of feet getting on and off an aircraft, how many individual human beings is that? The 'road warrior' who flies every week is at least 104 of those enplaned-deplaned passengers. In terms of social licence, upselling and customer retention, it's a good statistic to know and can be easily derived from survey data.

PEAK PERIOD FORECASTS

Hunter Harrison, former CEO of Canadian National Railways, once remarked 'don't build a church for Easter Sunday'[8] but annual traffic passenger forecasts will need to be broken down into projections of hourly and daily volumes to size facilities for the busiest travel periods.

A common approach is to construct a synthetic or nominal flight schedule for a busy day ten or twenty years hence, but this requires so many assumptions, and assumptions on assumptions, as to be of questionable value. Just imagine diarizing your daily schedule that far in the future. Benchmarking off larger airports with similar peak profiles can be helpful as can running sensitivity analysis on the current peak to base differential.

As with the Levels of Service concept, airports tend to accept the received wisdom here unquestioningly. The generally accepted rule is to plan for the 95th percentile day, that is, only 5% of the days in a year will be busier or, put another way, the airport will be overbuilt for 95% of the year. What is really required is a systematic assessment, consistent with the airport's strategy of the reduction in Level of Service that the airport is prepared to tolerate, or not, during peak periods.

In other words, the airport first needs to set business parameters around how it will manage peak demand rather than using a rule-of-thumb. Questions also need to be asked about the power of pricing to dampen peak load, use of temporary facilities or the possibility of attracting new business to fill the off-peak.

Finally, the question should be asked about how the peak period may change over the planning period? It's helpful to go back to the physics textbook and think about amplitude, the distance between peak and average and frequency, that is, the number of peaks per period. On the latter, the answer is 'probably not that much', absent a dramatic change in aircraft speed, although United Airlines has placed an order for the next generation of supersonic aircraft. Time zones are the great regulators here, for example, airports on the West Coast of North America tend to have early morning and lunchtime peaks for departures to the East Coast.[9] In terms of amplitude, peaks tend to spread partly because capacity constraints force air carriers into shoulder periods and as airports grow, they serve markets with different seasonal patterns. Finally, climate change could render winter travel peaks at airports serving ski resorts less pronounced or likewise arrivals at sunspots from northern climes in winter.

AIRCRAFT MOVEMENT FORECASTS

These are derivative forecasts based on the assumptions made about passenger volumes, aircraft size and load factors. To the passenger, air carrier movements need to be added freighter aircraft movements, which again is a derived forecast based on assumptions about the cargo market, which is covered in Chapter 5. The final piece of the puzzle is corporate and general aviation movements. Depending on the strategy of the airport, this can be a minor or major exercise.

For most large airports, the experience is that as they grow, get busier and become more expensive, corporate and general aviation will relocate to alternative airports. Nonetheless, it is one of the most challenging lines of business to forecast because airports have little direct exposure to it: they rarely own the facilities used by business aircraft, and the revenue from them, both landing fees and land rent, tends to be small compared to that from air carriers and other large tenants.

Warren Buffet famously quipped that business jets are both indefensible and indispensable. Use tends to rise in line with corporate profits but there are now counter-veiling forces such as impact on the corporate carbon footprint. The pandemic is another 'unknown' in that it's possible that companies will opt to fly in secure bubbles.

Looking at business aviation in Canada, shown in Figure 3.21, there is a strong correlation with corporate profitability over the period Q1 2004 to Q4 2018.

While there is a regular seasonal rhythm to business aircraft movements in Canada, corporate profitability is significant such that a 10% increase in net profit margin in corporate Canada produces a 9.5% increase in itinerant movements of many popular business jets. When we look at some of the lag effects, it is quite short: an increase in corporate profits in one quarter stimulates business aviation activity significantly and positively in the following quarter. Obviously, forecasting corporate profits out ten or twenty years is challenging but there is probably a linking relationship with GDP.

. . . .

Other Forecasting Techniques

STOCHASTIC FORECASTING

Linear regression is a deterministic approach, that is, if the economy grows by 1%, air travel will increase by 1.2%, with all other things being equal. It will tell you how closely the two are correlated and how much of the variation in demand is explained by the economy's performance; probably most of it, but some of the variation will be unexplained. That's why linear regression produces a straight-line forecast that can then be pressure-tested against various scenarios. Is there a methodology that

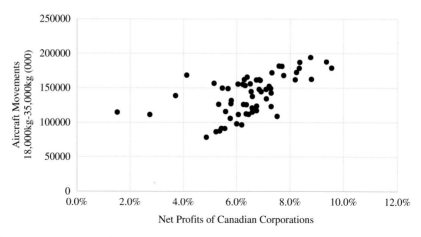

Figure 3.21 Business Aviation Forecasting.
Source: Statistics Canada.
Note: The data are from Statistics Canada. Net profit is from Quarterly Balance Sheet and Income Statement, by industry in Table: 33-10-0007-01 (formerly CANSIM 187-0001) and calculated as net profit over revenue as a percentage. The strongest correlation between net profits at Statistics Canada's many measurements of aircraft movements was with itinerant movements of aircraft between 18,000 and 35,000 kg MTOW from Table: 23-10-0023-01 (formerly CANSIM 401-0028). Into this category fall many popular business jets such as the Falcon 900 LX/EX and Challenger 350. The time period is quarterly from Q1 2004 to Q4 2018.

actually bakes in inflection points? Stochastic forecasting is one such approach in that it deliberately introduces some randomness because most systems, including air transportation, are complex. For example, a deterministic approach says: blue + red = purple, while a stochastic approach would say: blue + red = purple-ish, lavender or maybe a nice mauve.[10]

A linear regression model will say that the passengers using the airport in ten years' time will be x million assuming the economy grows at 2% per year. The stochastic model's output is stated in terms of probabilities, that is, there is a 95% chance that x million passengers will use the airport in ten years' time or, put another way, there is only a 5% chance that there will be more than x million.

Stochastic forecasting arguably produces better insights for management because it assigns a probability. A decision to plan for a certain number of passengers comes with, in effect, a warning label. A high growth scenario in a linear model is just the product of an assumption that the economy will grow at a faster rate but no explicit statement of the probability of that happening. Having said that, the stochastic model's inner workings are undeniably difficult to explain, even to a reasonably well-informed audience.

Forecasting should prompt spirited debate both within the airport itself and with business partners, stakeholders and the community. It's very easy for an airport to be put on the defensive in these discussions, almost as if its projections are under attack. A helpful way to frame these conversations is in terms of 'what you need to believe'. So, rather than getting into an arm-wrestle about whether the airport will be serving 40 million or 50 million passengers in ten years' time, re-frame the discussion to focus on the assumptions that lead to each outcome.

RELATIVE FORECASTING

How do we know if the airport is 'beating the market', that is, if its growth rate relative to the underlying economy is accelerating? This is a good marker of two things: changes in the structure of the economy so more air transportation is consumed per level of output and the airport's success in executing its strategic plan. In fact, it is really a warning light for an impending inflection point, one that is readily available and easily computed. We're using five-year intervals here to strip out some of the 'noise' in the data. Returning to the example of Amsterdam Schiphol, Figure 3.22 shows passenger volumes on the left axis and the ratio of the airport's growth relative to the Netherlands' economy on the right axis. As the latter improves, the passenger growth rate accelerates and vice versa.

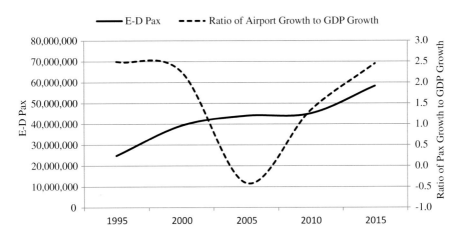

Figure 3.22 Amsterdam Schiphol's Growth Relative to Netherlands Economy.

Source: Schiphol Airport, Eurostat, Real Gross Domestic Product for Netherlands, retrieved from FRED, Federal Reserve Bank of St. Louis.

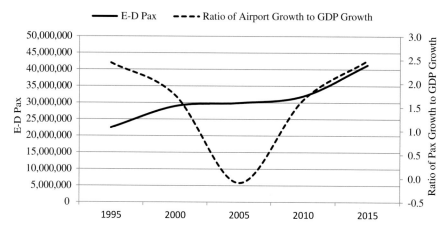

Figure 3.23 Toronto Pearson's Growth Relative to Canadian Economy.
Source: GTAA, Statistics Canada.

Another example, illustrated in Figure 3.23, is Toronto Pearson, which shows that a deceleration in the ratio of airport to economic growth preceded an inflection point to a slower rate of growth from 2000 to 2005 but then a pick-up pointed to an acceleration after 2010.

BIG DATA

In a seminal book,[11] Harvard data scientist, Seth Stephens-Davidowitz, made the compelling point that the opinion pollsters got it wrong on the election of Donald Trump and Brexit because people are not always candid when interviewed. However, (aggregate) Internet search patterns do not lie and Google and other search engines helpfully allow us to track public interest in issues or topics. A singular advantage of using search volumes is that they are available weekly with almost no delay. We have used several examples of this in the book already.

Figure 3.24 tracks global Internet search volumes for the term 'Travel Visa' and international passengers at a selected group of global hub airports. The search term is a reasonable proxy for interest and intent to travel internationally and the two lines track very closely. In fact, the Internet search patterns are a 'digital canary in the coal mine' because when search activity picks up, it manifests itself in passengers showing up at airports two months later.

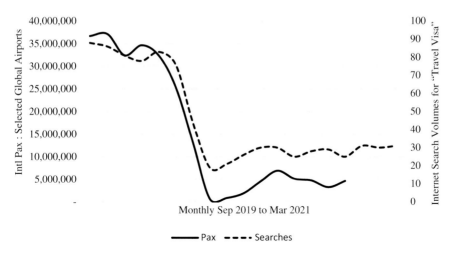

Figure 3.24 Consumer Interest in Travel Visas.

Source: Google Trends, Various Airports.

FORECASTING AND THE PYRAMID OF PLANNING

Just as the Pyramid of Planning helps alignment, so does consistent forecasting. It is not uncommon for plans with shorter time horizons to use different forecast assumptions, possibly because the future is more visible but often it's just a lack of resources or organizational discipline. It is undeniably challenging to re-knit these disparate assumptions about the future into a seamless forecasting 'jumper'.

In any event, enplaned-deplaned passenger volume may not be the best forecast metric for short-term planning, as shown in Figure 3.25. Depending on the precision required, the real drivers of operating revenue, operating income and net income may well be aircraft movements, because landing and terminal fees are based on 'the metal' and international passengers, particularly non-residents, because of their high propensity to spend in retail and duty-free concessions and be accompanied by greeters and well-wishers, boosting short-term parking revenue.

EXTERNAL SHOCKS

A special sub-set of inflection points are external shocks such as the 9/11 terrorist attacks, SARS or the Great Financial Crisis of 2009 which affect

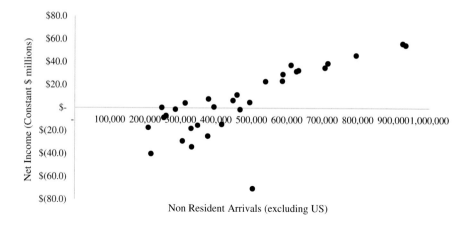

Each dot represents one quarter from Q1 2010 to Q4 2017

Figure 3.25 Quarterly Net Income and Residents of Countries Other Than the US Arriving at Toronto Pearson International Airport Each Dot Represents One Quarter from Q1 2010 to Q4 2017.

Source: Calculated by author from publicly available data from the Greater Toronto Airports Authority and Statistics Canada.

the whole industry and depress demand for a period. Because they come from outside the industry, we refer to them as 'external' and they usually have a global impact.

We can measure external shocks is in terms of a shock severity index which is simply the size of the drop in passengers from peak to trough multiplied by the time to recover to pre-shock demand levels. So, simply put, it is the size of the drop multiplied by the length of the recovery. Table 3.1 shows the Airport External Shock Severity Index of the recent events.[12]

Table 3.1 Airport External Shock Severity Index

Shock	Duration	Peak to Trough (% change)	Time to Recover (years)	Shock Severity Index
9-11/SARS	2000–2004	–9.1	4	36
Great Financial Crisis	2008–2010	–4.1	2	8

This helps us put Covid-19 in perspective; its impact is already orders of magnitude greater than the industry has experienced.

Summary and Conclusions

Almost all airports' growth trajectories follow an S-curve with inflections caused by any number of factors including air carrier hub strategy, aircraft engine technology, exchange rate fluctuations, market deregulation or the airport's success in expanding its catchment area or increasing its share of a connecting market. Think of these inflection points as signals, as distinct from the noise of short-term oscillations.

A series of geographical lenses needs to be applied. Where is the airport on the global propensity for air travel curve and are there other national and regional airports that are leaking or siphoning traffic?

Because forecasts drive facility requirements, they are usually produced by sector (domestic vs international) and by itinerary (origin-destination vs connecting). Peak period forecasts are necessary too, but a strategic overlay and an abundance of caution should be exercised when projecting these far into the future. Forecasting is also about understanding the customer, so other outputs can be more market-based including resident vs non-resident demand and by frequency of travel. These segmented outlooks may also have stronger correlations with financial performance and can help stitch together the Pyramid of Planning.

Assigning probabilities to outcomes helps decision making, and can build broader support for the airport's strategy, but the methodology to do so is not without its challenges.

Cross-checking forecasts with those of other components of the air transportation system, air carriers and air navigation authorities can be helpful too. Debates internally and externally can be more productive if framed in terms of 'what you need to believe' as opposed to a zero-sum 'we are right, and you are wrong' type of exchange.

Tracking an airport's growth against the economy is a readily tracked and computed warning light for an inflection point either due to the changing nature of the propensity for air travel or the success (or otherwise) of the airport's strategy.

In any event, models will need to be recalibrated post-pandemic as air travel patterns and propensities change. This is an opportunity for a broader refresh of the science and art of forecasting, for example, using Big Data as a digital canary in the coalmine.

Despite all this, many airports still show straight-line forecasts in a Master Plan to determine the timing and scale of expansion. Think of the traditional straight-line forecast as the base of a soup, that is, necessary but bland and not particularly nourishing. It is only when potential inflection points are thrown into the pot does it become appetizing and useful, with scenarios and probabilities as the croutons on top.

This chapter has dealt with passenger forecasting. Cargo forecasts are dealt with in Chapter 5.

NOTES

1 Extended Range Twin-Engine Operational Performance Standards aka 'Engines Turn or Passengers Swim'.
2 Buffalo Niagara International Airport, Sustainable Master Plan Update, 2013, Niagara Frontier Transportation Authority.
3 We measure the size of an economy by its gross domestic product or GDP. This is simply the total value added in an economy in a year. To use a very simple example: you own a forest, you cut down some trees and sell them to a lumber mill. The value added is the difference between what you paid for the forest and what the mill pays you for the raw wood. The mill then processes the raw wood into lumber and the value added is the difference between what the mill paid you for the trees and the price paid by the home builder for the lumber, and so on through millions and millions of daily transactions.
4 This is shown on a log-scale which simply means it shows the percentage increase. A steeper line means a larger percentage increase.
5 At the countries' major airport: Sao Paulo (GRU) in Brazil and Kuala Lumpur (KUL) in Malaysia.
6 Calgary (YYC) or Vancouver (YVR).
7 Great Financial Crisis 2008–2010.
8 As told in Green, *Railroader*.
9 Assuming a five-hour flight time and three-hour time zone difference, aircraft need to leave the West Coast by 1,300 hours to arrive on the East Coast by 2,100 in time for connections to the last bank of departures.
10 Reddit ELI5: the difference between deterministic and stochastic.
11 Stephens-Davidowitz, *Everybody Lies*.
12 Peak to trough decline in pax for selected global hub airports.

BIBLIOGRAPHY

Green, Howard. *Railroader: The Unfiltered Genius and Controversy of Four-Time CEO Hunter Harrison.* Vancouver, BC, Page Two Books Inc., 2018.

Niagara Frontier Transportation Authority. *Buffalo Niagara International Airport Authority Sustainable Master Plan Update – Final Technical Report,* Buffalo, NY, 2013.

Reddit ELI5: The Differnce between a Deterministic and Stochastic Model: explainlikeimfive (reddit.com), 2021.

Stephens-Davidowitz, Seth. *Everybody Lies: Big Data, New Data, and What the Internet Can Tell Us about Who We Really Are,* New York, NY, Bloomsbury, 2017.

4

MASTER PLANNING FOR PASSENGERS

INTRODUCTION

In the previous chapter, we talked about demand and how airport management can identify and prepare for the next inflection point or indeed induce it themselves. The next step is to convert that demand into facility requirements. This factor may be called the 'coefficient'. For each process or facility at the airport, for example, the space required for pre-board screening, the number of gates and retail space, three questions need to be asked:

- how might this coefficient change in the future?
- what is the likelihood that this activity will migrate off-airport?
- can pricing alter the demand?

Traditional master planning will say, in essence, that if forecast for the horizon year is 40 million passengers, the 'black box' will say that the airport will need a terminal building with x square metres of space and y number of gates. The black box could be a simple ratio from benchmarking against other airports or it could be more sophisticated analysis with terminal gate plots drawn up for a hypothetical schedule of flights on a peak day in the future.

'There is a many a slip between cup and lip' is an apt saying here meaning that between the demand forecast and facility requirements, much can change. That is why we need to ask the three questions or, put another way, open up the black box and unpack the many assumptions, including about Level of Service, contained within it.

DOI: 10.4324/9781003173267-4

Translating Demand into Supply

COEFFICIENT CHANGE

In answering this question, an airport should reflect on its strategy and can also ask how <u>it</u> wants to change a coefficient. In other words, not only external technological or business forces are at work here. There is a story[1] about Hunter Harrison, the former CEO of Canadian National Railways, who early on in his tenure was presented with a plan to expand CN's inter-modal yard at Brampton, Ontario, just north of Toronto. The plan entailed a considerable capital expenditure. After hearing the presentation Harrison remarked, in colourful language, that there was no need to expand the yard, it just needed to be operated more efficiently. If trains could be made up and broken down quicker and cars unloaded faster, there was plenty of capacity. In other words, coefficient change can come from a strategic decision to squeeze more productivity out of existing assets.

Coefficient change also resembles an S-curve, as we will see as we move through this chapter. The shift in customer behaviour from checking in at the airport to doing so online has not been linear one, nor is the incidence of mobility impairment by age group.

Airside

One of the best examples of this is the increase in the numbers of passengers per aircraft movement, we have witnessed over the last ten years. In other words, the coefficient by which passenger demand is converted in aircraft movements has changed substantially with the effect that runways have become more productive and the need for new ones deferred.

This was a widespread phenomenon: from 2010 to 2015, 81% of airports worldwide had an increasing number of passengers per movement. In North America, 77% airports had rising passengers per movement and the average growth rate is 7%. In Europe, 38 out of 39 airports had growing passenger per movement with average growth rate of 41%. The passenger per movement rate grew by an average of 10% at 70% of airports in Asia.

The 'upgauging' story has two parts: bigger aircraft and more people on them. In 1995, the average departure by a US air carrier had 111 passengers on it; by 2019, that had increased to 153. So, in a little over 20 years, the normal time horizon for a master plan, the coefficient by which passengers get converted into aircraft movements increased by 38%. In fact, if we look at Figure 4.1 closely, we can actually see two phases. Between 1995 and 2007, average aircraft size did not change very much but load factors increased but then roles were reversed between 2008 and 2019. Arguably, the Internet gave air carriers the ability to price seats more sharply to fill their planes, after all, that unsold seat is the ultimate perishable product. Possibly, that advantage was fully exploited by 2007 after which the 'metal' just had to get bigger.

Master plans developed between 1995 and 2010 did not always anticipate this trend and so recommended earlier construction of new runway capacity. For example, the Toronto Pearson International Airport Master Plan of 2008 anticipated the need for a new runway by about 2030 but the updated 2017–2037 plan expects that passenger demand can be met on the existing runway system because further increases in passengers per movement are expected to materialize.

Once the industry has emerged from the pandemic, there are several scenarios for the passengers per movement coefficient. It could go down if passengers develop a preference for non-stop flights to avoid crowded hubs and additional Covid-19 screening processes. Some passengers may feel more comfortable travelling with members of their personal or corporate 'bubbles', boosting corporate aviation. New runway construction could feature amongst stimulus projects to get the economy moving again, removing the capacity constraint that can drive upgauging. The coefficient could also go up, for example, if air carriers shrink the business-class cabin as some of that demand has migrated permanently to Zoom, Teams and Skype or carbon taxes incentivize

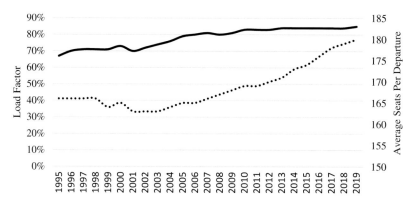

Figure 4.1 Aircraft Size and Load Factors.
Source: MIT Airline Data Project.

the use of bigger, fuller aircraft on trunk routes that generate fewer unit GHG emissions.

From this, we convert a passenger forecast into an aircraft movement forecast, together with projections for all cargo aircraft, discussed in Chapter 5, and business and general aviation.[2]

Terminal

There are many coefficients to size of terminal buildings including the level of service the airport's strategy calls for, the type of passengers, for example, leisure versus business and the 'peakiness' of demand but a central one is the interface between the terminal and airside systems, that is, the number of passengers processed through each gate. We are going to refer to this as the gate utilization rate and we should note here that a 'gate' includes a jet bridge attached to the terminal building, a walk-out apron stand or a remote stand accessed by bus. A high productivity airport will get about five aircraft turns per day on a gate.

Many factors drive this coefficient the share of connecting passengers, the share of international passengers, air carrier business model and terminal configuration. Larger airports just have higher gate utilization simply because there are just more flights over a day at bigger airports. Independent of airport size, passenger per movement drives this coefficient up as more larger planes enplane and deplane more people while not necessarily occupying a gate for a proportionately longer time. The international share decreases gate utilization because international arrivals and departures windows are less 'elastic', that is, dictated by time-zones, curfews, slots and connecting flows. The terminal configuration coefficient shows us that airports with more than one terminal or where terminals are divided into two or three sectors have lower gate utilization rates because a domestic gate may be empty, but the flight arriving is from overseas and cannot use it. Finally, for low-cost carriers, fast turns are an integral part of their business model.

Post-pandemic process to sanitize aircraft could well increase turn-around time. One study concluded that it could require between 10% and 20% more ground time.[3] Other, similar changes may include 'socially distanced' boarding and Covid-19 test checks.

Of course, other benefits come from higher gate utilization rates. Total operating expenses are reduced and concession spending per passenger increases because a steady flow of passengers throughout the day underwrites a critical mass of shops and restaurants offering a better range of products and services, open for longer hours.

What can an airport do in the short-term to drive up gate utilization? Co-operation and data-sharing (A-CDM)[4] between the entire airport community can support on-time performance and efficiency. Some airports are moving towards a common-use model for stands and equipment: pooling of ground handling equipment meaning less need for the manoeuvring of vehicles to load and unload, strict enforcement of stand allocation rules, data sharing between airport and air carriers and deploying innovation to improve turnarounds such as Artificial Intelligence (AI). Necessarily, airports need to have some buffer gates for irregular operations and for unplanned repairs. To reduce the buffer, AI will allow airports to analyse data on past performance from sensors on jet bridges, better predict when it is going to fail and take preventative action. Pricing that incentivizes quick turns is also an option, but it has not been widely adopted.

Passenger security screening is a process with many ramifications for terminal planning with throughput ranging between 100 and 300 passengers per hour per lane. In other words, a lot more capacity can be squeezed out of the real estate by low-cost operational changes. A detailed study undertaken by researchers at Imperial College, London revealed that the key ingredients to success were long lanes, multiple loading positions, auto-tray returns, a high supervisor to staff ratio, real time data analytics to better match staff to demand and publicly declared or regulatory imposed targets for screening time. Unsurprisingly, airports with lower wait times and higher lane throughput are also more cost efficient. Today, the person screening the contents of baggage is doing so at the airport, usually at a monitor beside the lane the passenger is moving through but there is a future where the contents of the bag are examined remotely at centralized bunker serving the whole country.

Ground Access

In the previous chapter, we talked about the disruption underway in the urban mobility market with declining rates of automobile ownership and the rise of the TNCs[5] such as Uber and Lyft and the impact these trends are having on airport parking revenues. The common thread is the greater utilization of vehicles that would otherwise be parked.

A second imperative in ground access planning is reducing GHG emissions, all of which will reduce the amount of parking and curb space required per passenger. For example, depending on the fuel source, one of the least sustainable forms of ground transportation is picking up or dropping off of passengers by automobile as it entails a deadhead trip, that is, you return from or travel to the airport 'empty'. Over time, this will likely be discouraged by a combination of pricing, access control and changing social attitudes. The pandemic and the ability to say goodbye virtually may also reduce the incidence of greeters and well-wishers, dampening the demand for short-term parking.

Finally, vehicle access to the terminal may be curtailed to prevent terrorist attacks or other criminal activity such as organized theft from baggage carousels or human trafficking.

A long time series of data at a large sample of airports are not available to analyse this but we can look at the impact of rail links which an estimated 223 airports have of which 71 have opened since 2010.[6] We find that airports with rail have total asset bases that are 2.5% smaller, controlling for all other factors, due to the lower investment required in access roads, terminal frontage and parking lots.

Another metric to look at is the mode-split, that is, the share of passengers using the train. Many factors drive this including overall rates of urban density and car ownership, for example, Europe is different to North America in that respect, distance to the CBD, frequency of service and how well the airport rail line is connected to the rest of the regional network just to mention the main ones. To give some idea of the coefficient change that can be induced by a rail connection, the share of passengers using public transit at Vancouver International Airport (YVR) changed from 4% before rail rapid transit service started to 25% ten years later.

Aviation Fuel

The footprint of aviation fuel infrastructure is significant including storage tanks, truck racks[7] and pipelines. The amount of fuel stored at an airport is a function of several factors including security of the supply chain, for example, if a single pipe is delivering fuel, then a larger a reserve must be on hand in case of an outage, compared to a situation where there are multiple delivery channels. As Figure 4.2 shows, US air carriers reduced the amount of fuel need to fly one seat mile by 25% between 1995 and 2019 and if we assume there will be further efficiencies as aviation drives to net zero GHG emissions this should reduce amount of land devoted to fuel storage tanks at a given traffic level.

Demographics

A final source of coefficient change will be the passengers themselves, particularly in parts of the world where the population is aging and mobility impairments rising. In short, it will take more resources for

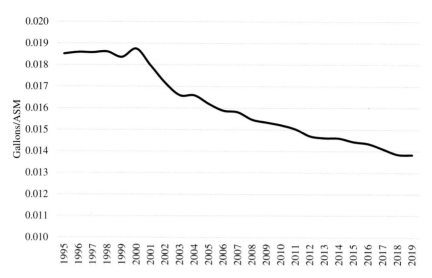

Figure 4.2 Aircraft Fuel Efficiency.
Source: MIT Airline Data Project.

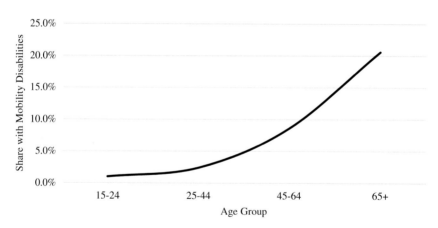

Figure 4.3 Incidence of Mobility Impairment.
Source: Statistics Canada, Canadian Survey on Disability, 2012, 89-654-X.

these passengers to navigate the usual airport processes. According to data from the United Nations[8] by 2050, one in six people in the world will be over age 65 (16%), up from one in 11 in 2019 (9%) while one in four persons living in Europe and Northern America could be aged 65 or over. In a classic S-curve shown in Figure 4.3, the incidence of mobility impairments reaches 20% in the 65 and over age group. This could increase the number of passengers with mobility impairments by 38% over the next 30 years.[9]

ON-AIRPORT/OFF-AIRPORT

We could write a list of things we used to do at the airport, which would include, for example, check-in, dropping our bags and shopping all of which have become 'distributed' to varying degrees.

Off-airport check-in and bag-drop has been around for a long time but still required the customer to go to a particular place, for example, an Airport Express MTR station in Hong Kong. We now check in at our own desk, or on our phones, and sure enough when we look at internet searches for airline online check-in, shown in Figure 4.4 back to 2004 as a proxy, we see an unmistakable S-curve. Please note that the inflection point on the right predates Covid-19, in other words, online check-in was routine by 2019.

Terminal planners in the early 2000s probably oversized check-in concourses. This is a good time to recall Bill Gates' maxim that people tend to overestimate the amount of change in that will occur over three years but underestimate change over ten years. Our planners probably saw a few early adopters checking in online but not very much change in three years it was taking to prepare the plan but ten years on, it was the passenger checking in at the airport that was the exception.

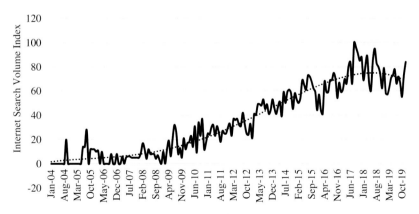

Figure 4.4 Consumer Interest in Online Check-In.
Source: Google Trends.

We used to carry our bags to and from the airport; however, services have emerged that will pick up your baggage at your office, home or hotel and deliver it to the airport for direct induction into the baggage system. You do not see it until you arrive at your destination. To avoid the crush around the baggage carousel in a post-Covid world, there may well be a viable business in delivering it to you at home. Other possibilities include sending your baggage in advance by FedEx, for example.

Chicago Midway Airport (MDW) recently announced that passengers will be able to order food for delivery in the terminal from the restaurant of their choice.[10] So, assuming this is successful and becomes widespread, the amount of terminal space devoted to food preparation will decrease, all other things equal.

PRICING

Prices are wonderful things: they alter behaviour. The assumption about the number of checked bags per passenger is a fundamental input to terminal planning and the propensity to check a bag fell when airlines started charging in 2008. While we do not have data on the volume of bags checked or carried on, we can look at internet search patterns as a proxy for consumer behaviour and, as Figure 4.5 shows aggregate

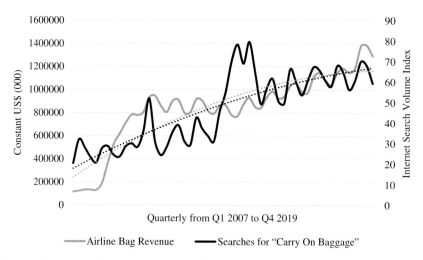

Figure 4.5 Checked Bag Fees: Key Trends.

Source: Google Trends and US Bureau of Transportation Statistics.

revenues that air carriers earn from baggage fees and consumer interest in carry-on baggage in response. The light grey line shows that airlines introduced fees for checked bags in 2008 and it shows the expected seasonal patterns. We have stripped out the effect of inflation. The black line is consumer interest in carry-on bags represented by Internet search volumes in the US for that term.[11] Some of these searches will be consumers thinking of purchasing a carry-on bag and some for what is allowed on a plane but we are using it as a proxy for a change in passenger behaviour. There is a strong correlation (0.70) between the two. We only have US data but every 10% increase in aggregate airline bag revenue, produces a 7.2% increase in searches for carry-on baggage which, put another way, is telling us that 72% of passengers have the option of not checking a bag while the others are either not price sensitive or have no choice but to check a bag.

Another example of using pricing is to reduce vehicle traffic in the terminal area. Phoenix Sky Harbor International Airport (PHX) recently revised its charges for commercial ground transportation providers to encourage drop off and pick up at a transit station on the periphery of the airport where passengers can take a people mover (the PHX Sky Train) to the terminal building.

Pricing can also be effective in discouraging corporate and general aviation at major airports. Landing fees are generally weight based, so smaller aircraft pay less even though they may be using a runway slot which may otherwise be occupied by a wide-body jet or they result in a wide spacing of aircraft on approach to meet wake separation standards. A useful rule of thumb here is to compare the cost of parking a car for a day in the CBD and landing a corporate jet. If that latter is less than the former, landing fees are too low.

SUPPLY

OPTION IDENTIFICATION

Having determined the land and facilities necessary by multiplying the demand forecast by the coefficients to translate it into supply, we now get to the identification and evaluation of options phase. Suppose that the determination is that 20 additional gates will need to be added to the terminal. What exactly and where do we build them? Do we add them as remote stands, or to existing piers, build a new pier, or build a new terminal? If so, do we so to the west or to the east? What gauge do we build?

Invariably, there will be several options to, for example, expand the passenger terminal, build a new runway, construct a new highway link or locate a fuel farm. Some will be well entrenched and have powerful advocates. Indeed, careers may have been built on it. However, rarely is there a 'silver bullet', a solution that's so clearly advantageous over the others that makes it the obvious choice; in fact, beware of this kind of ammunition. So, it's advisable to cast a broad net here and avoid a rush to judgement. An airport can even invite business partners, stakeholders and the community to identify options which means relinquishing some control over the planning process, but it builds engagement and legitimacy. Some proposals will be clearly fall into the wildcard category; however, the evaluation criteria will flag these.

OPTION EVALUATION

There is no 'right' answer; only an informed choice with the trade-offs made explicit and the engagement of all concerned but inevitably there is a rush to judgement about which option is best, possibly from the loudest or most senior voices in the room. This is how airports make mistakes, sometimes very expensive ones. So, you will need a framework and process to analyse the performance of each option against a series of criteria.

Outwardly, this may appear laborious, even pedantic, but this is how you flush out trade-offs, issues and concerns that may otherwise be overlooked given the inherent complexity of an airport. There's no reason why business partners, stakeholder and the community cannot be asked to suggest evaluation criteria and participate in the evaluation process. By engaging these groups, they now have ownership of the plan and even though the final options selected may not be their preferred ones, the process has been open and transparent which tends to mute the opposition.

One framework for the evaluation matrix is sustainability which would include economic, environmental, social and governance criteria. Table 4.1 shows a concrete example of this employed by Vancouver Airport Authority in the development of the 2007–2027 Master Plan.

Governance criteria cover the consistency of each option with the airport's mission, vision, values and objectives, whether it creates business opportunities, for example, the creation of an innovation cluster and finally and importantly does it preclude other development options? It was this criterion that led to a rapid transit line at YVR being built at grade so as not to preclude a crossover taxiway being built over it.

Table 4.1 Evaluation Criteria 2007–2027, Vancouver International Airport Master Plan

Governance	Economic	Environment	Social
MVVO*	Capacity	Habitat aquatic	Vehicle traffic
Opportunities	Capital cost	Habitat terrestrial	Archaeology
Preclusions	Passengers	Rare species	Recreation
	Business partners	GHG emissions	Social benefits
	Government agencies	Air quality	Economic impacts
	Cargo interface	Water quality	Aircraft noise
	Security/health	Land use efficiency	Community response
	Operating costs		
	Revenue		
	Delivery time		
	Risk		
	Flexibility		
	Redundancy		

Source: Vancouver Airport Authority, updated by author.
Note: *Mission, Vision, Values and Objectives.

The economic criteria cover the basics of how much capacity does the option deliver and at what cost? Including capital and operating costs ensure that the full life-cycle cost impact is considered. Then, it looks at the likely reaction and preferences of passengers, business partners, including air carriers, and government agencies. For example, the latter generally prefer consolidated operations and so will like the option of one international terminal not two or more. Air carriers like consolidation too and ideally want to operate in one, multi-sector terminal with their alliance partners. This increases the productivity of staff and equipment and shortens minimum connecting times, which makes the hub more competitive. Retail and duty-free operators will prefer aggregated flows of passengers and fewer large stores than many small ones.

The cargo interface criterion captures the location of the passenger terminal relative to current and future cargo terminals (for belly cargo) and relative to runways and highways to ensure an efficient supply chain. For example, air carriers such as FedEx and UPS think in terms of minutes, so long or unreliable taxi or ground access times impair their performance and that of the regional economy.

Security and health really address the ability to secure and isolate the facility, for example, multiple pre-board screening points mean that re-screening after a breach is more manageable compared to a centralized model. Planning and design to mitigate the risk of a terrorist attack would fall into this criterion too. The importance of public health in the post-pandemic world probably means this deserves its own set of criteria including the ability to isolate passengers and flights from others.

The final set of economic criteria look at the risks associated with construction, for example, does the option involve building in an active operating area or is it on a greenfield site? Flexibility speaks to the potential to repurpose the space based on a multitude of potential futures including regulatory and technological changes or to construct it in a modular fashion based on different demand scenarios while redundancy is the ability of the airport to function if the facility is taken out of service, for example, due to a fire or accident.

The environmental criteria are largely self-explanatory with land use efficiency designed to capture and reward options that result in mixed-use or higher density development.

Social criteria refer to the impacts on surrounding communities including vehicle traffic and aircraft noise. Archaeology is there to assess the impact of the option on, for example, ancient burial grounds. The recreation criterion is designed to capture options that may, with little additional cost, become community assets, for example, a new bike trail built adjacent to a new rapid transit line or a park at the end of an extended runway. The social benefit of air travel is intended to capture some of its intangible benefits of such as connecting with an extended network of family and friends while the economic impact criterion picks up jobs, taxes and value-added generated by the airport either in the aggregate sense or from the execution of the particular project. The concept of economic impact can be extended to include employment opportunities for target groups. Community response is a 'catch-all' to gauge the likely controversy that a particular option may generate.

Let's look at an evaluation matrix in action. In its 2007–2027 Master Plan, Vancouver Airport Authority carried two options for the third runway: on the foreshore to the west of the airport or one parallel to the existing south runway on the main body of Sea Island, as shown in Figure 4.6.

In governance terms, the foreshore runway scored higher because it opened potential new business opportunities such as a marine terminal and industrial land and did not preclude other development options. The economics were clear: a runway on the foreshore would cost considerably more than the south parallel but because it would operate independently from the existing two runways, it delivered more capacity. It was longer so could accommodate more types of aircraft as well as offering a buffer if climate change increases summer temperatures, degrades aircraft performance and necessitates a longer TODA.[12] However, the foreshore runway would take more time and be riskier to build and have a much greater environmental impact too because it would intrude into

FORESHORE RUNWAY

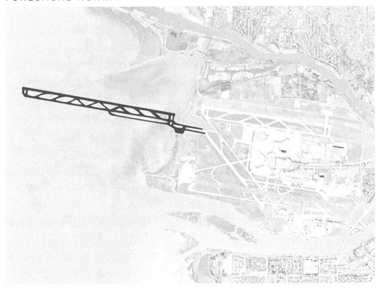

SOUTH PARALLEL (SHORT) RUNWAY

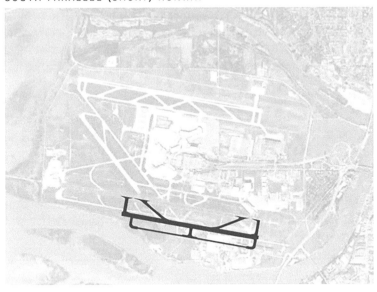

Figure 4.6 Principal Airside Options: 2007–2027 Vancouver International Airport Master Plan.

Source: Vancouver Airport Authority, 2007–2027 Master Plan.

sensitive terrestrial and aquatic habitats. However, on the social criteria, it was quieter. Moving the runway took it further away from residential communities.

The two options created an economic, environmental and social trilemma. The most economically advantageous option imposed more noise on surrounding communities, while the quieter runway came with a significantly larger price tag and environmental impact.

The long gestation periods for runways raises the question of interim uses on land that is reserved for them. The opportunity cost of this can be high given the availability of alternative airports, ground access modes for short-haul trips and imperative of revenue generation. For example, Toronto Pearson International Airport referred to its plan for a major public transport hub at the airport as its 'fifth runway', that is, by improved regional rail access would free up capacity for long-haul flights to emerging markets, better connecting Toronto to the world.

Meaningful differences between the performance of options on all criteria cannot always be discerned in which case they can be scored equally or not at all. It's also understood that the data to measure and score performance may be incomplete or estimated.

Suppose the initial round of option identification has resulted in a bucket of possibilities; you can start with a coarse screen to whittle down the number of options to a more manageable number of contenders and then put them through a finer sieve such as the example showed here.

HIERARCHIES

Once the land required for the basic building blocks of an airport: runways, taxiways, passenger terminal and ground access has been identified, we need to establish some principles for how the residual land should be allocated. The land requirements of each category should generally be met in descending order.

OPERATIONAL HIERARCHY

1. Essential for the safe operation of aircraft: air traffic control, fire hall, airfield maintenance, de-icing facilities, hangars.
2. Essential for efficient air carrier operations: fuel, cargo, catering, ramp equipment storage, maintenance, waste management.

3. Other aviation-related services: aircraft manufacturing and mainten-
    ance, business aviation.
4. Ancillary services for passengers: car parking, hotels, car rentals.
5. Aviation-dependent uses: industries that are not necessarily aviation
    related but exhibit a high propensity to travel or ship cargo by air:
    national or global corporate headquarters, pharmaceutical companies.

With respect to aviation-related uses, some will require land and direct
access to a runway or taxiway, generally referred to as airside land but
others will not. Airport land that does not have direct access to a runway
or taxiway, generally referred to as groundside land, has traditionally
been occupied by businesses that are still 'aviation-related', e.g., facilities
supporting rental car operations at the airport, flight kitchens and aviation
fuel tanks but just does not need a direction connection to the taxiways and
runways. Airside land generally commands a premium over groundside
land, on the order of 10%–15%, because there is a finite amount of it.

   One of the biggest planning mistakes an airport can make is locating
a groundside aviation-related use on airside land, for example, fuel farms
do not need direct airside access as aircraft do not pull up like it's a gas
station. This speaks to the importance of the Pyramid of Planning in
aligning subordinate plans, for example, one for commercial land development with the Master Plan.

   The fifth category, aviation-dependent uses, is a new one and speaks
to the 'beyond the boundaries' theme of this book. Traditionally, airports
have been home to aviation-related businesses and clearly any business
that requires direct access to the runways and taxiways will locate an
airport, e.g., aircraft maintenance, general and corporate aviation facilities, air cargo. In many jurisdictions, airports are restricted by law to
'aviation-related' land uses through official plans and zoning ordin-
ances. The analysis presented here suggests that the traditional distinction between 'aviation-related' and 'non-aviation-related' may longer be
helpful and that we can contemplate new category which we refer to as
'aviation dependent'. These are businesses that are large consumers of
air passenger and freight transportation services and place a premium on
proximity to an airport accordingly. In terms of regional economic competitiveness, it's desirable to accommodate and enable these businesses.

   Several years ago, a global industrial auction company approached
Vancouver Airport Authority to construct a head office building at the
airport for the simple reason that their business required extensive air
travel and it was more productive for them to be located as close to the
airport as possible. This is a classic example of an aviation-dependent

use. In the end, the project did not proceed for other reasons. Another example of an aviation-dependent company that would benefit from an on-airport location is a food manufacturer in Vancouver, BC, specializing in Matsutake mushrooms, grown in the forests of north-western British Columbia and popular in Japan because of their purported aphrodisiac qualities. The manufacturer had to collect the mushrooms flown down from the north at Vancouver International Airport, transport them off-airport for cleaning, processing and packaging before heading back to the airport for enplanement on a flight to Tokyo.

So, the optimal regional approach would be to ensure that the lands at or close to an airport, that are not required for aviation-related uses are occupied by those industries with the greatest need for proximity to air transportation services. Ordinarily, one would expect the market to do this, but if there are regulatory prohibitions that prevent 'aviation-dependent' businesses from locating at an airport because they are not deemed to be 'aviation-related' in the traditional sense, then there is an inefficient land allocation.

FLOW HIERARCHY

Then consider a flow hierarchy to guide how uses are co-located on the airport.

1. On airside, minimize crossings of controlled surfaces by ground vehicles and aircraft under tow and potential runway incursions.
2. On groundside, consider the trip generation rate of facilities to minimize travel times and emissions.

If cargo tugs, fuel and catering trucks or other ground service equipment (GSE) must cross runways, taxiways or aprons, it means constant communication with air traffic control and the potential for delay and miscommunication. Towing aircraft across active runways should also be avoided too.

The number of vehicle trips generated by different land uses varies greatly, for example, a business park generates an average of 0.42 trips per thousand square feet of gross leasable area compared to 1.72 trips for an intermodal truck terminal.[13] The trip generation rate of a business park may be further reduced to the extent that ride-sharing, cycling and public transit options are available. Another example is fuel storage facilities which can be sited in the 'back-forty' as only a handful of people will work there.

LAND USE PLAN

All of this will ultimately manifest itself in the form of a Land Use Plan for the airport where areas will be coloured according to permitted use. Typically, areas will be identified and reserved for long-run expansion of the airside, terminal and ground access facilities with land allocated for operational support, such as fire halls.

In terms of land zoned for commercial development, there is a constant tug-of-war between having narrow or broad definitions of uses to maximize flexibility, particularly if there is a lengthy consultation and review process to change designations. Land generically zoned as 'groundside commercial' can create disquiet in adjacent municipalities that the airport may want to develop a non-airport related retail mall. Not all airside commercial land is created equal either. For example, an airport was under pressure to build more aviation fuel storage tanks. The best, long-term solution would be to locate them deep in the airfield which is secure environment and public do not need access to them. However, that would entail costly servicing, so a piece of prime airside commercial land, facing onto a runway, is selected instead. Not only that, but the metal tanks ended up interfering with the Instrument Landing System, requiring expensive mediation.

Cross-hatching is a device that can be used where the deployment of land could be to two potential uses but it can also muddy the waters further.

The challenge is how best to assure fealty to the Master Plan which, in turn, depends on the processes necessary to change it. If an airport is self-regulating, the short-term lure of a development project and cheaper servicing costs can lead to sub-optimal long-term decisions. This is why sub-area plans, in the middle tranche of the Pyramid of Planning, are necessary to bridge the gap between a set of broad land use zones in the Master Plan and specific development projects.

CROSS CHECKS

SENSITIVITY ANALYSIS

Having identified and evaluated a number of options, you will be in a position to make recommendations; however, before doing so, it's prudent to undertake a number of sensitivity analyses. If the recommended options perform well under different scenarios, they are more robust.

In all probability, you will be working within a range of forecasts. How sensitive is the option should a lower rate of growth materialize? For example, what is the risk of asset underutilization?

Similarly, you will have made assumptions about coefficients, so, for example, how do the airside options perform at a lower or high rate of passengers per movement? For example, the passenger per movement rate may not resume its upward march, post-pandemic, as passengers opt to fly in smaller, less full aircraft. Does that advance the addition of new airside capacity or increase the demand for corporate aircraft terminals? Or, what if gate occupancy times increase due to stricter sanitation protocols or slower, more socially distanced boarding processes. Will that advance the timing of the need for more gates?

Another sensitivity test is to weight the evaluation criteria differently. The starting assumption is that each one is equally important but loading them differently to reflect current political climate or the centrality to the airport's strategic plan can add insight. For example, if the airport aspires to become a hub airport, more emphasis could be placed on criteria that reflect the needs of the hub carrier and connecting passengers. So, the air carrier or alliance-based terminal concept may score higher. Alternatively, if aircraft noise or GHG emissions are pressing issues, then weight the relevant criteria more highly, so the options that minimize both perform better.

BENCHMARKING

Having determined the facility and land requirements, it's helpful to benchmark them against other airports.

We're going to use a comprehensive data base of 200 airports around the world ranging in size from Atlanta, Georgia (ATL) at almost 100 million passengers to Dunedin, New Zealand (DUD) at just under 1 million. This data base is compiled by the Air Transport Research Society (ATRS) for 2015 and includes data on revenue, costs, traffic and assets, for example, terminal floor area and number of gates, using standardized definitions and all reported in US dollars.

What explains the total asset base of an airport? Unsurprisingly, it is the volume of passengers and the relationship is strong and linear such that a 10% increase in passengers translates into a 9.7% increase in assets. So, an airport's asset base essentially moves in lockstep with passengers and the correlation is a strong one: total passenger volume explains 75% of the variation in airports' asset values.

There are regional patterns: in North America and Asia-Pacific, a 10% increase in passenger produces a 9.4% increase in total assets but in Europe, the increase is 11.1%. One possible reason is that European airports are more land constrained, expansion is more expensive and subject to measures to mitigate its impact.

If we look at size-bands, when airports with less than 20 million passengers have a 10% increase in passengers it results in a 9.5% increase in assets while above 20 million, it is 10.2%. This is not a huge difference, but it suggests there is something of a step change above which expansion becomes more expensive due to the complexity of large airports.

A good master planning rule of thumb is that the percentage increase in total asset value contemplated in the master plan should be broadly consistent, in real terms, with the forecast percentage increase in passengers. So, your proposed facility requirements, converted into costs, should not deviate significantly from the trend line in Figure 4.7.[14]

In other words, if the projected asset base of the airport having executed its Master Plan ends up 75% bigger but passenger volumes are forecast to grow by 25% then something is wrong.

We are not only interested in the quantum of total assets but the return to them.[15] As Figure 4.8 shows, at any given passenger volume, there is a wide range of asset endowment and because we are looking at a snapshot, some of this may be due to an airport having recently undergone a substantial expansion or is poised to do so. The other explanation

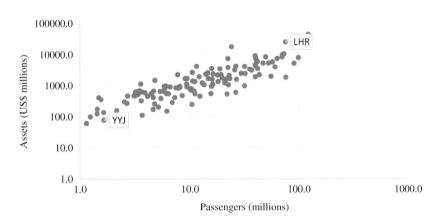

LHR = London Heathrow, YYJ = Victoria International Airport, BC, Canada

Figure 4.7 Traffic Volumes and Asset Bases LHR = London Heathrow, YYJ = Victoria International Airport, BC, Canada.

Source: Author's calculations using Air Transport Research Society (ATRS) 2015 data base.

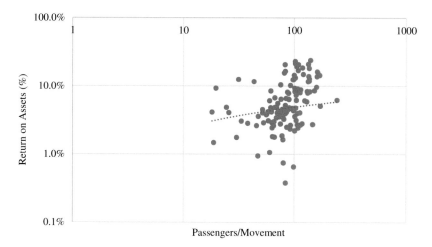

Figure 4.8 Airport Productivity and Return on Assets.

Source: Author's calculations using Air Transport Research Society (ATRS) 2015 data base.

is that some airports have simply planned better and driven up their return on assets (ROA).

One observation we can make about return on assets is that we do not see a correlation between airport size and ROA. So, size does *not* matter.

Runway and terminal buildings make up a large proportion of an airport's asset base and bigger, fuller planes mean higher utilization rates of both. We capture this in the passenger per movement rate and as Figure 4.8 shows there is a positive correlation with returns on assets.

THINKING ABOUT THE PASSENGER

Most Master Plans are organized by facility type, so there is a chapter on airside, then one on passenger terminals and one on ground access. But passengers do not experience the airport that way; it's one journey from curb to cloud. Not only that but it involves all three components of a transportation system: the terminal, the vehicle or the way. For example, the passenger sitting on a plane waiting for a gate after a ten-hour flight is indifferent as to whether the delay is due a shortage of controllers, work-to-rule by the air carrier's ground crew or a broken airport gate.

How do we put the passenger at the centre of the Master Plan? One way to do so by recalling the oldest saying in transportation is 'moving passengers are happy, stalled passengers are unhappy'. While each company along the passenger's journey will have its own set of performance measures and which may well all say 'we put the passenger first' they're not comparable or public. Indeed, they probably measure success within the organization's boundaries, but not outside them. For example, 'the airport was sparklingly clean, but I waited at Customs for sixty minutes'. So, while each one may report a successful year, that's scant consolation for our passenger stuck on a plane.

Fortunately, we have a consistent, passenger-focused metric, namely, on-time performance (OTP) which is defined as an arrival or departure within 15 minutes of schedule. It has been measured consistently across many airports for many years by OAG.

Figure 4.9 shows that while passenger per movement drives up return on assets, it drives down on-time performance.

This is not the place for an exhaustive discussion, but many things explain an airport's OTP. In some cases, it may just be having a bad year, for example, labour unrest, construction or IT system failures or its dominant carrier is. Interestingly, weather is not a factor because airports adapt, for example, in cold, snowy places they tend to become very good at de-icing.

OTP worsens as airports get bigger, specifically, a 10% in total passengers results in a 0.4% reduction in OTP, while a 10% increase in passengers/movement, independent of size, results in a 11% deterioration.

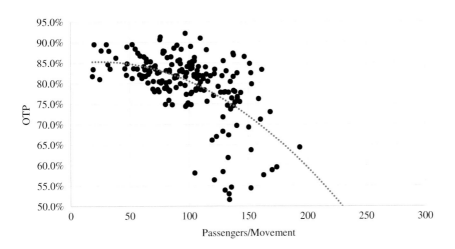

Figure 4.9 Airport Productivity and On-Time Performance.

Source: Author's calculations using OAG and Air Transport Research Society (ATRS) 2015 data bases.

Both factors, total passengers and passengers per movement, explain just over one-third of the difference between airports.

A high incidence of belly cargo tends to reduce OTP because loading an aircraft is more complicated. All the passengers and bags are on board and ready to depart but there has been a hiccup in the cargo sheds. A 10% increase in the share of total WLUs represented by cargo reduces OTP by 1.9%.

Not in all cases obviously but there are just more things that can go wrong and less spare capacity for recovery as airports get larger and planes get bigger and fuller.

So, while passengers per movement increases return on assets, it also depresses OTP which can adversely affect an airport's brand and long-term competitiveness. A Master Plan needs to aim for the sweet spot.

SUMMARY AND CONCLUSIONS

Demand gets translated into supply by way of coefficients such as passengers per aircraft or passengers per gate. These coefficients are dynamic and evolving, in fact, coefficients follow the same S-curve trajectory that we saw in overall passenger demand but traditional master planning does not always make this explicit.

The three questions to ask are: how could this coefficient change in the future, could this task take place off-airport and could pricing moderate demand? Just because it has always taken 90 minutes to deplane, cater, fuel and enplane a Boeing 737 does not make this a safe planning assumption going forward. Boarding time could increase with verification of pre-flight Covid-19 tests and social distancing requirements, so gate utilization goes down. Or, biometric boarding checks could increase it. Common-use ground service equipment (GSE) could mean the necessary vehicles are always stationed at the gate, regardless of air carrier or ground handler and any number of the many tasks associated with turning an aircraft could be automated or, using AI, made more efficient. In other words, coefficients are not like your grandmother's chocolate cake recipe, handed down unchanged from generation to generation.

It is really a tug of war between forces that will increase the coefficient like centralized screening of carry-on bags in a bunker thousands of kilometres away, against those that will decrease it such as the higher incidence of mobility impairment in an ageing population. It's quite possible that it ends up as a draw, but you have to go through the process.

Having looked at various demand and coefficient scenarios, the next phase in a Master Plan to identify land and facilities needed to supply that demand. To avoid the pitfalls of the 'obvious' solution, an evaluation framework is essential to consider all the options' performance on many facets and identify rationally, deliberately and collaboratively, the best performers.

Later in the process, sensitivity analysis can be applied to test the Plan under different traffic growth and inflection scenarios. Benchmarking against other airports can ensure the asset and passenger growth are broadly consistent and offer a sense check on optimizing the competing demands of return on assets and customer experience, as captured by on-time performance.

NOTES

1. As told in Green, *Railroader*.
2. Business aviation is historically correlated with corporate profitability although post-pandemic coefficients may change as companies may opt to fly in 'bubbles'. There are subtle synergies with scheduled service. Linamar, one of Canada's leading auto parts manufacturers based in Guelph, Ontario reported that international connectivity was so good at Toronto Pearson that they rarely used their corporate jet for overseas trips.
3. Schultz et al., "Future Aircraft Turnaround".
4. Airport Collaborative Decision Making.
5. Transportation Network Companies.
6. Data from Global Air Rail Alliance (GARA).
7. Where fuel is decanted into trucks.
8. United Nations, 2019 Revision of World Population Prospects World Population Prospects – Population Division – United Nations.
9. Assume today there are 1.0 million passengers of which 15% are over 65 (US numbers) and 20% have mobility impairments equals 30,400 passengers but by 2050, 21% of passengers are over 65 with the same 20% mobility impairment rate equals 42,000 passengers or an increase of 38%.
10. Davitt, "Midway Partnership".
11. The spike in searches in early 2014 is probably due to United Airlines announcing new restrictions on the size of carry-on baggage.
12. Take off distance available for a given aircraft and payload.
13. Institute of Transportation Engineers, *Trip Generation Manual*.
14. Log scales are used because of the large range of numbers in the sample and it illustrates the percentage change in total assets with respect to passengers.
15. Defined as NOI/total Assets.

BIBLIOGRAPHY

Davitt, Dermot. "Midway Partnership and Grab Launch Mobile Food Ordering Service in Chicago". The Moodie Davitt Report. Accessed March 29, 2021. https://www.moodiedavittreport.com/midway-partnership-and-grab-launch-mobile-food-ordering-service-in-chicago/.

Green, Howard. *Railroader: The Unfiltered Genius and Controversy of Four-Time CEO Hunter Harrison.* Vancouver, BC, Page Two Books Inc, 2018.

Institute of Transportation Engineers. *Trip Generation Manual*, 10th ed., Washington, DC, Institute of Transportation Engineers, 2020.

Schultz, Michael, Jan Evler, Ehsan Asadi, Hennings Preis, Hartmut Fricke, and Cheng-Lung Wu. "Future Aircraft Turnaround Operations considering Post-pandemic Requirements". *Journal of Air Transport Management* 89 (October 2020): 101886. https://doi.org/10.1016/j.jairtraman.2020.101886.

5 MASTER PLANNING FOR CARGO

INTRODUCTION

Air cargo[1] does not rent cars or buy duty-free; it does not send e-mails complaining about the cleanliness of the washrooms and tends to operate from sheds, out of sight, out of mind of the airport's leadership team. Historically air cargo has been an afterthought, for example, cargo terminals are often operated by third parties and by extension, airports do not make very much money off cargo or, consequently, collect very much data on it.

Air cargo actually is a misnomer and we should really think of it as freight that is transported by air for all or part of its journey. Undoubtedly this is the most challenging line of an airport's business to forecast.

Some air carriers have become increasingly detached from the cargo business. Not only have many of them outsourced the physical handling of air cargo to third-party ground handlers but many have sold their cargo capacity in bulk to global freight forwarders such as Kuehne and Nagel or Panalpina and only have a peripheral knowledge of the actual shippers and receivers. Because a box of widgets does not care if it takes a circuitous route to its destination, the business can be opportunistic. That is, spare capacity may be deployed to attract cargo that would otherwise have no reason to route through a particular airport. An example of this would be a company shipping engine parts from Shanghai, China to Dusseldorf, Germany. The shipper will put the matter in the hands of its freight forwarder who determines that the least expensive way of getting these parts to Germany on time is to truck them to Hong Kong, fly them to Amsterdam and then by truck again to Dusseldorf. So even though this shipment is actually air cargo between PVG and DUS, it does not show up in either airport's enplaned-deplaned tonnage.

In many respects, cargo is a harbinger for the future of airport planning. It's a highly competitive business, packages do not care about

DOI: 10.4324/9781003173267-5

routing and it is truly multi-modal in the sense that the majority of the cargo processed at some airports does not actually see a plane. Finally, while the physical enplaning or deplaning of cargo still takes place at the airport, the electronic processing of it for Customs purposes often does not. To refer to Porter's Five Competitive Forces, cargo tends to have more substitutes and the number of airports competing for the business is greater.

Not to put it too finely, cargo is agile and volatile and it can be challenging for many airports to get their arms around it, particularly those that are more focused on passengers. However, the pandemic has revealed its critical nature in delivering PPE, pharmaceuticals and, more broadly, responding to households' swift transition to online shopping.

Given the complexity and ever-shifting nature of supply chains, cargo is one area where engagement with business partners is critical. In this regard, airports need to move beyond 'dumb tonnes', challenging though that can be, and know what goods are moving through the facility, understand the supply chains and build relationships with those involved and another example of airport planning moving beyond the boundaries.

Finally, a word about terminology. When we refer to passenger air carriers, these are ones that carry cargo in the bellies of aircraft but also may have all-cargo aircraft in their fleets. When we talk about integrators, we mean air carriers like FedEx, UPS or DHL that have completed integrated, door-to-door operations. The final set is ACMI carriers,[2] for example, Atlas Air that operate on aircraft on behalf of other air carriers and are the tramp steamers of the air cargo world.

DEMAND FORECASTING

After most of the forecasting budget has been spent on passengers and aircraft movements, many Master Plans make a cursory attempt to project cargo volumes and the associated aircraft movements, usually by some simple extrapolations or benchmarking.

GLOBAL

As we saw with passenger travel, the propensity to ship by air is correlated with the economic development; specifically, as incomes grow from $5,000 to $15,000 per capita, the demand for air freight increases dramatically.[3] The relationship is such that a 10% increase in GDP per capita translates into a 17% increase in air freight per capita. There are several reasons for this including the transition from a primary to a goods and services-based economy, integration into global supply chains and rising incomes so people and businesses can afford to the ship and receive by air.

What is interesting in Figure 5.1 is the position of certain countries. For example, Kenya is above the trend line partly because of the large volumes flowers shipped by air to Europe while the Netherlands' position reflects the global cargo carrier and hub airport status of KLM and Schiphol Airport (AMS). South Korea is a manufacturing, export-oriented economy with a national carrier specializing in cargo[4] while the potential for growth in India is evident.

NATIONAL

Looking at a national picture, we will use the US as an example since it has the most comprehensive and accessible data. Figure 5.2 shows changes in the volume of freight shipped by air, rail and truck over the last 20 years.

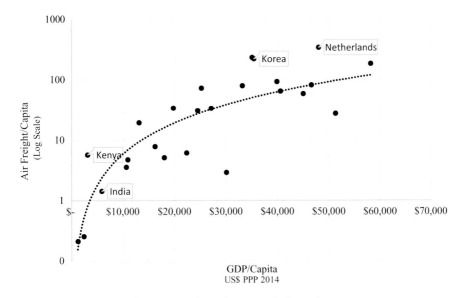

Figure 5.1 Propensity for Air Freight and Economic Growth.

Source: Author's calculation from Airports Council International (ACI) and IMF data.

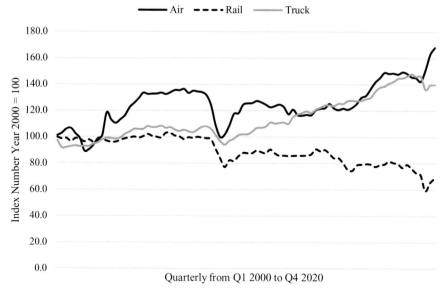

Figure 5.2 Freight Volume by Mode.
Source: Economic Research Division; Federal Reserve Bank of St Louis.

After the bursting of the 'Dot Com Bubble' in 2000 and the terrorist attacks of 9/11, air freight demand picked up quickly before contracting during the Great Financial Crisis of 2009. Growth resumed however and demand levelled off at a lower level. It accelerated again in late 2016, decelerated in 2019 and then the Covid-19 pandemic hit and growth took off.

Two further observations: air and truck freight demand is strongly correlated[5] and air freight appears to be more sensitive to economic conditions as witnessed by the magnitude of its contraction during the GFC compared to rail and truck cargo. In fact, before the pandemic, the demand for air freight is about three times more responsive to changes in the economy than truck or rail borne freight.[6]

For passenger air carriers and ACMI carriers, the ecosystem of specialized facilities, handlers, agents and brokers at global hub means that they are essentially captive to these airports. When we look at a selection of these[7] and compare passenger and cargo trends over the last 25 years, we see a divergence after 2010, as shown in Figure 5.3, when passenger growth outstripped cargo at an increasing rate. Possible reasons for this include air carriers cramming more passengers into planes which means there is less payload available and, second, the integrators'

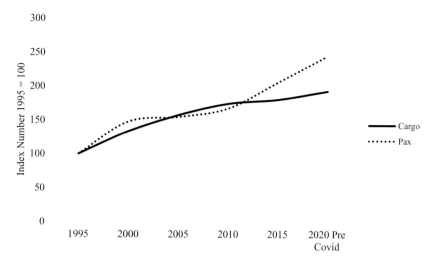

Figure 5.3 Cargo and Passenger Airports at Key Global Hub Airports.
Source: Author's calculations from various airports' websites, ACI, Wikipedia.

share of the total air freight market has increased. For example, FedEx and UPS ranked fifth and seventh in international freight volumes in 2012 but had climbed to third and fifth, respectively, by 2018.[8] Finally, this may reflect the relatively faster growth of 'south to south' trade[9] which is bypassing these global hubs which, with one exception, are in the Northern Hemisphere.

REGIONAL

Forecasting should be done at a regional level. Cargo is footloose, even restless, and can more easily relocate to secondary airports as its infrastructure demands are less, packages won't complain about a longer ground access trip and it is a very cost sensitive business.

If we look at South East England, 83% of the region's air freight arrives and departs from London Heathrow (LHR), the vast majority in the bellies of passenger aircraft. In contrast, at London Stansted (STN) and London Luton (LTN) which process 13% of the region's air freight, virtually all of it arrives and departs on all-cargo aircraft.[10] Slot constraints at Heathrow (LHR) and because these airports are less congested, all-cargo aircraft have based themselves there, for example, Luton is a spoke for DHL. Actually, it is a very rational allocation of scarce runway capacity around London.

Another example is from Canada where the majority of cargo in Southern Ontario is processed at two airports, Toronto Pearson Airport (YYZ) and Hamilton International Airport (YHM). At Pearson, it's carried on a mix of belly and all-cargo aircraft while at Hamilton, it's virtually all freighters. As Figure 5.4 shows, an inflection occurred at YHM in the period 2007–2010 when a number of companies, for example, UPS, Purolator, DHL and Cargojet relocated from Toronto Pearson in search of lower costs, less congested ground access and 24-hour operating capability. Consequently, the proportion of cargo carried on freighters at Toronto Pearson fell from 49% in 2005 to 36% in 2018.

In the San Francisco Bay Area, the secondary airport, Oakland International (OAK), is dominant in cargo with 53% of the region's enplaned-deplaned tonnes in 2019 compared to 16% of enplaned-deplaned passengers.[11] Oakland is FedEx's West Coast hub and is closer to the industrial centre of the Bay Area than SFO, now that computers are made in China, not Silicon Valley, and software is downloaded, not installed from a disk in a package.

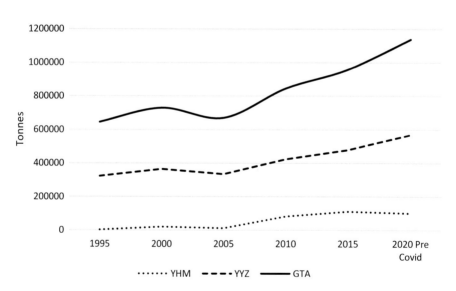

Figure 5.4 Cargo at Southern Ontario Airports.
Source: Statistics Canada.

Multi-Modal

You may have read about astronomers seeing a 'wobble' in the aura of a distant star confirming there's an unseen planet orbiting it. Forecasting cargo volumes at an airport is little like that because we can't see inside the sheds where increasing volumes of cargo processed at on-airport facilities arrive and depart by a truck and never see the hold of an aircraft.

Our 'wobble detector' is looking at employment in air freight and related business around airports and comparing that to the reported enplaned-deplaned tonnes.[12] At Manchester International Airport (MAN) in the UK, employment in air freight transportation and related services[13] around the airport[14] increased by 500% between 2015 and 2019, mainly due to the opening of a large Amazon warehouse but enplaned-deplaned tonnage only grew by 8.1%. Around East Midlands Airport (EMA), there was a similar pattern: a 37.2% increase in employment[15] on a 15.4% growth in cargo being loaded and unloaded from aircraft.

A puzzle at Vancouver International Airport (YVR) for many years was that enplaned-deplaned tonnes in all-cargo aircraft, mainly FedEx and UPS, were flat but the land devoted to and employment in cargo, as measured in economic impact studies, had increased.

In other words, planning cargo facilities based on enplaned-deplaned tonnage alone will not capture the role of the airport in a multi-modal supply chain and undersize the land required and ground access for trucks and employees.

Inflection Points

As pointed out in the passenger demand forecasting chapter, we see inflection points, that is, changes in the 'wiring' that alters the trajectory of growth, for example, Figure 5.5 shows the share of US retail sales online by quarter since 2010. In other countries, for example, the UK and China, the penetration of online shopping is greater. While not quite an S-curve, the slow, steady increase in the share suddenly spikes during the pandemic and will likely settle at a higher 'resting' rate. Tangible evidence of this is Amazon establishing its own cargo airline and associated facilities.

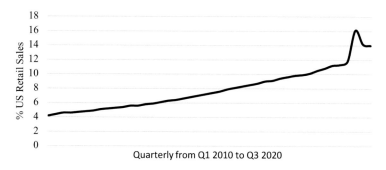

Figure 5.5 E-Commerce Trends in the US.

Source: U.S. Census Bureau, E-Commerce Retail Sales as a Percent of Total Sales

In fact, when we regress this against the air freight index shown earlier, we find that the rise of e-commerce explains about one quarter of the increase in volume over the period.[16]

DIRECTIONALITY

Unlike passenger volumes which tend to balance out directionally over time, the same is not necessarily true for cargo. For example, flowers shipped from Africa to Europe during winter are a one-way flow or because a stronger currency will induce more imports (deplaning) and depress exports (enplaning) (Figure 5.6).

If we look at Sydney, Australia, we see an inflection point in 1995 after which the rate of growth in international freight slowed but also that a significant bi-directional imbalance emerged in 2000. Inbound freight started to outstrip outbound volumes with the widest gap in 2010. This is explained by the strength of the Australian dollar which peaked that year when it 'only' cost A$0.92 to buy $1.00 US. Imports were relatively cheap and inbound international freight volumes were therefore high.

DISTRIBUTED

As noted in the introduction, air cargo will be physically handled at the airport, but it may not necessarily be processed there. The number of freight forwarders and customs brokers in Richmond, BC,

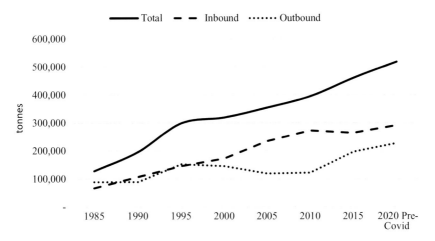

Figure 5.6 Directionality of Air Freight.
Source: Commonwealth of Australia, BITRE Data Base

where YVR is located increased by 15% from 2004 to 2013 but those located at the airport declined by 28%.[17] There are various reasons including more competitive rents, electronic customs clearance and the multi-modal nature of the business. Freight forwarders and customs brokers in Richmond no longer need to locate at an airport and, in fact, there is a cluster adjacent to provincial highway, a Class A railroad and seaport.

FORECAST OUTPUTS

SUB-MARKETS

One way to think about it is concentric rings of cargo demand with descending degrees of 'stickiness' to an airport. In the innermost ring is origin-destination cargo from shippers of products with a high value to weight ratio that means they are almost always shipped by air. Diamonds would be an example or perishable products such as seafood or flowers. In the next ring would be the same category of goods that will connect through the airport because it's the most convenient hub. The next ring would be origin-destination cargo that may be shipped by air if the price is right. Airports' cargo catchment areas can be vast, to the point of being meaningless. For example, because of the wide range of direct services to Europe, and a low Canadian dollar making it an attractive for US shippers, Air Canada will truck freight 800 km from Chicago to Toronto. Finally, the outer ring would be connecting cargo which is transiting an airport for purely opportunistic reasons.

FREIGHTER CARGO

Freighter borne cargo volumes tend to be closely related to regional economic conditions. For example, the correlation between enplaned-deplaned tonnes at YYZ and Canada's GDP is only 0.55 but at Hamilton (YHM), the predominantly all-cargo airport, it's 0.92 which is very strong.[18] Likewise, the correlation between the performance of the UK economy and cargo volumes at East Midlands Airport (EMA) is stronger at 0.94 compared to 0.83 at LHR where belly cargo dominates.[19] Once the nature of that relationship is established, a base forecast can be made off long-run economic projections.

In terms of forecasting freighter aircraft movements, an understanding of how the major integrators, for example, FedEx and UPS work is essential. Packages flow to and from these companies' major sort hubs at Memphis, Tennessee; and Louisville, Kentucky, respectively, or sometimes regional hubs. The 'Big Sort', as it is known, sees hundreds of aircraft arriving between approximately 20:00 hours and midnight and departing between 02:00 and 06:00. As volumes increase, arrival and departure times will not change but larger aircraft will be deployed and eventually some regional demand will splinter off and be carried in smaller aircraft.

BELLY CARGO

Belly cargo is opportunistic. The payload available for cargo on a passenger aircraft is relatively small and air carriers will always prefer to carry another human being because they yield much more revenue, even after they have been fed, watered and otherwise attended to, for an equivalent weight.[20]

Across a sample of 200 airports, we see that as the passenger per movement rate increases, cargo volumes decrease. At LHR, for example, we see that the correlation between cargo and passengers is strongest in the off-peak months of Q1 and Q4 but weaker in the peak seasons of Q2 and Q3 which suggests that cargo capacity gets sacrificed when passengers need it.[21]

We can forecast the demand for belly cargo using a residual approach, that is, by estimating the capacity left after passengers, bags and fuel have been accounted for.

To illustrate this approach at a micro-level, let's look at a B777-200 flying 5,271 km between Toronto (YYZ) and London (LHR).[22] The two weights critical to aircraft operations are: maximum take-off weight (MTOW) which for this aircraft is 247,200 kg and its operating empty weight (OEW) of 134,800 kg. The former is the weight above which the aircraft simply will not get off the ground and the latter is its weight without any passengers, cargo or fuel on board. So, the difference is the payload available of 112,400 kg. The weight of the fuel for this mission plus a 10% reserve is estimated at 57,600 kg.[23] Assuming 400 seats and an 85% load factor, that means 340 passengers and their bags which will collectively weigh about 35,700 kg.[24] The residual available for cargo is estimated at 19,100 kg or 17% of the total payload available.

Complicating matters further is that cargo capacity is stated in cubic terms and it's possible that this flight carries its maximum capacity, 163 cubic metres, but it consists of upmarket feather pillows that only weigh two tonnes. In other words, an aircraft can 'cube out' before it 'weighs out'.

For these reasons and if cargo data are unavailable or incomplete, a simple rule of thumb can be used. Let's use the concept of a workload unit (WLU) as a common unit of measurement of passengers and cargo. Simply put, one WLU is equal to one passenger *or* 100 kg of cargo, the theory being that the average passenger weighs 100 kg. So, for example, an airport with 10 million enplaned-deplaned passengers and 1,000,000 kg of cargo translates to a total of 10,100,000 WLUs.[25] Looking across a sample of 200 airports of all sizes and all regions and excluding those that specialize in cargo,[26] passengers represent an average of 90% of total WLUs.[27] The rule of thumb is that if the forecast is for 50 million passengers, then the cargo volume would be expected to be 556,000 tonnes.[28] If we compare that to the freighter forecast, then we can net out the belly cargo share.

Of course, we are making several assumptions about coefficients remaining constant which may not be safe, particularly post-pandemic. For example, a greater percentage of the aircraft may be devoted to cargo if passenger demand remains depressed or the yield gap, which favours passengers over cargo, may narrow. These scenarios can be easily modelled.

BENCHMARKING

The correlation between passenger and cargo volumes is a strong one, as illustrated in Figure 5.7 so if a cross-check of the forecasts for cargo and

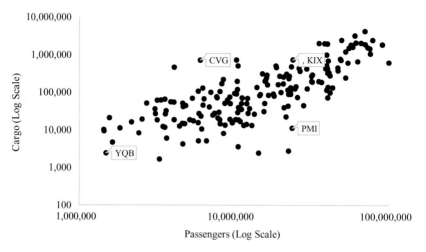

Figure 5.7 Relationship between Passenger and Cargo Volumes.

Source: ATRS 2015 Data Base. Airports predominantly in the cargo business, for example, MEM, SDF, ANC and LUX excluded.

passengers is significantly out of line, then questions need to be asked. There may however be perfectly legitimate explanations for outliers such as Quebec City (YQB) which is served by turboprop aircraft with little cargo capacity.[29] As we saw earlier, Cincinnati (CVG) lost its passenger hub status but is now a hub for Amazon and one of three global hubs for DHL. At the 24 million passenger level, we have Palma di Majorca (PMI), a tourist, low-cost carrier airport reporting only 11,000 tonnes of cargo but also Osaka (KIX) processing 745,000 tonnes because it is an international airport in an export economy served by wide-body aircraft.

TRANSLATING DEMAND INTO SUPPLY

COEFFICIENTS

There are some comprehensive studies and manuals on cargo facility planning and it is not intended to replicate these other than to itemize the main points.

Productivity of cargo facilities is measured by annual tonnes per square metre (ATPSM), but it varies due to factors including international versus domestic volumes, storage times, automation, the peakiness of demand, special handling requirements, for example, security, sanitation or refrigeration and, finally, the type of cargo, for example, reasonably standard packages or items of disparate size, weight and volume. A common-use cargo building will likely be more productive than an exclusive use one so the business model will have a bearing too. Based on a detailed study,[30] a rule of thumb for sizing cargo buildings in North America would be about 10 annual tonnes per square metre. However, if land is scarce, much higher ATPSM rates can be achieved in common-use, multi-storey facilities such as at Hong Kong International Airport (HKG).

The space needed to park aircraft in front and trucks at the back means the floor area ratio (FAR) for cargo buildings is low: in the 0.15–0.25 range, that is, the building area will be between 15% and 25% of the total land area.

This leads to some very different potential requirements for land and cargo buildings, as shown in Table 5.1, for example, an airport processing 500,000 tonnes of cargo per year in a high productivity building and with a high FAR, because aircraft are parked further away or there is relatively little trucking or employee parking could do so on 10 ha. of land but it could be as high as 100 ha. in other circumstances.

Another factor to consider is that all-cargo aircraft operate on a different daily cycle to passenger aircraft with longer dwell times, increasing the need for parking stands per movement.

FLOW CONSIDERATIONS

For planning purposes, facilities processing belly cargo need to be within reasonable proximity of the passenger terminal while integrator terminals are more 'footloose'. However, the two worlds are not hermetically sealed from each other, for example, FedEx will put freight on a regular passenger aircraft if it makes business sense to do so.

Minutes matter! Consider Seattle, Washington, located at the northwest corner of the lower 48 US states. Non-stop flying time to FedEx's

Table 5.1 Cargo Building and Land Requirement Scenarios

Assuming 500,000 tonnes annually

Building Processing Rate (ATPSM)	Cargo Building Area (m2)	Floor Area Ratio (FAR)	Land Area (ha)
5.0	100,000	0.10	100
10.0	50,000	0.15	33
15.0	33.333	0.20	17
20.0	25,000	0.25	10

Source: Author's calculations.

Super Hub at Memphis, Tennessee is approximately three hours and Memphis is two hours ahead of Seattle. For the plane carrying Seattle's packages to reach the Super Hub by 23:00 hours, it must leave SEA by 18:00. That means chocks-off at 17:45 to allow for taxiing and runway delays, so the van carrying the packages from all over Seattle must arrive at the airport depot by 17:15 at the latest. Traffic is usually snarled on I-5 from Downtown Seattle to the airport, so FedEx may have to impose a 15:30 cut-off for package pick-up, which means companies have less time to finish that critical document or machine part and get it reliably to their customer in, say, Miami the next day. DHL ships packages from its hub at Leipzig, Germany for 08:00 delivery to offices in Central London to Luton Airport while it envelopes with a guaranteed delivery time of 14:00 get flown the DHL's main UK hub at EMA and then are trucked up to London.

The point being is that the location of express cargo facilities needs to be finely calibrated to minimize ground access and airside time, to benefit the regional economy as a whole.

THINKING ABOUT THE SHIPPER

BEYOND 'DUMB TONNES'

Just as we introduced the passengers into the Master Plan in Chapter 4, this is where we can insert the shipper. When we understand who is moving what through the airport, we can begin to understand the role the airport plays in the supply chain for those companies and industries from which we can build relationships and contribute more meaningfully to their success.

Most national statistical agencies report exports by value and port of departure which can be a good place to start. Insights into what is being carried, and why, can sharpen forecasting.[31]

We know that the value-to-weight ratio of goods shipped by air is high. The kinds of goods shipped by air include perishables such as food and plats, precious metals and stones, pharmaceuticals and advanced manufacturing products.

The differential will vary over time and between different countries: these data are for Canada where a considerable volume of bulk resources such as coal, potash and grain are shipped by rail so depressing the average value-to-weight ratio, but Figure 5.8 shows just how big the margin is.[32]

To state these numbers in terms of the prices we pay at the supermarket, air freight is lobster, rail is basmati rice and truck is ground coffee.[33]

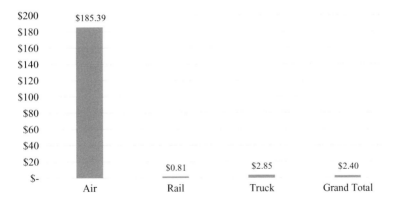

Figure 5.8 Value-to-Weight Ratios by Mode.

Source: Government of Canada, Canadian Centre on Transportation Data, Table 23-10-0142-01.

If we think about air freight as the 'lobster' of goods movement, it reminds us of the premium placed on the value of time and the security and integrity of the supply chains at airports. The same cannot be said for rail as if you watch a freight train roll by in Canada, you cannot help but be struck by the sheer volume of graffiti adorning the cars.

Case Study: Exports by Air from Alberta, Canada

The Canadian province of Alberta is home to two international airports, Calgary (YYC) and Edmonton (YEG) which, in 2019, served 18.0 million and 8.2 million passengers, respectively.

In terms of the conventional measurement of cargo, in 2019 there were 89,000 tonnes enplaned and deplaned at YYC and 27,000 tonnes at YEG, so Calgary is a 3.3 times larger cargo airport, by weight.

When we look at the value of exports through each airport, we get a very different picture with Calgary processing 13.3 times more value at $2,913.6 million compared to $219.6 million at Edmonton. A large part of the difference is the $1,256 million worth of diamonds, the ultimate high value-to-weight ratio item, being shipped via YYC from the Northwest Territories to Belgium and India for cutting. Even when we net out diamonds, the value of goods exported by air through YYC is still larger than YEG by a factor of 7.6.

If we just look at exports by air that originate in Alberta, YYC accounts for 71% of the total value and YEG 10%. Significantly, 10% travel by truck 1,200 km to YVR and 8% do likewise 3,300 km to YYZ. In other words, YVR is as important an airport for Alberta exporters as

YEG, probably because of the greater choice of non-stop international flights there. For airports wanting to understand how much local air cargo is 'leaking', these data are invaluable.

Finally, in terms of understanding supply chains, the data reveal that just under $10 million worth of live breeding swine were exported from the adjacent province of Saskatchewan to Russia via YEG.

STIMULATION

Additional belly capacity can redirect some existing business, but it also has a stimulative effect. IATA reports that a 1% increase in air cargo connectivity is associated with a 6.3% increase in total exports and imports.[34] Figure 5.9 shows an example of this: the change in value of Canadian exports by air to China after non-stop flights between Toronto and Beijing started.

SUMMARY AND CONCLUSIONS

The pandemic has revealed the importance of air cargo, not only in terms of the distribution of PPE and vaccines but also in contributing the airports' bottom lines. Cargo volumes have fallen by less than passengers

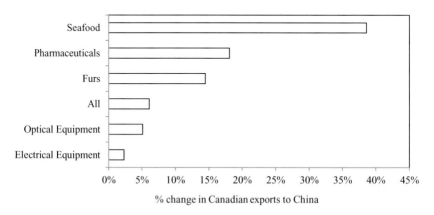

Figure 5.9 Market Stimulation.

Source: Statistics Canada, GTAA, Author's calculations.

and, going forward, cargo will be a more important contributor to airport and air carrier profitability. For example, it could make the difference between a route being viable or not.

Air cargo is agile, volatile and valuable: think of it as the lobster of the freight universe. Volumes are very sensitive to economic conditions. It moves on routings and by modes that make the most sense for the price point and delivery commitment rendering traditional definitions of catchment areas redundant. The supply of more wide-body passenger capacity can redirect and stimulate cargo demand while the tramp steamers of the aviation world, the ACMI carriers, can quickly fill any supply gaps. Longer-term integrators such as FedEx and UPS can defect to secondary airports, all of which makes forecasting challenging.

Best practice for cargo forecasting can be summed up by the saying 'think globally and act locally'. So, it includes a global perspective in terms of the propensity to ship freight by air and a regional one because of air cargo's footloose nature in the short-term and long-term.

Engagement with business partners and going beyond 'dumb tonnes' is necessary to understand what goods and the supply chains that the airport is part of, recognizing that this is easier to do at large international airports where there is a paper trail of export and import forms but more challenging at smaller domestic airports.

Planning facilities based on enplaned-deplaned tonnes will likely undersize them because airport cargo buildings will often process more cargo that arrives and departs by truck than by plane. There is also a wide range of land and building productivity scenarios to consider, influenced by many factors. The 'circadian rhythms' of all-cargo aircraft are different to passenger aircraft, so they can sit on the ground much so that the coefficient translating aircraft movements into parking positions is higher.

On the airport, minutes matter for express cargo and the suboptimal location of facilities relative to highways and runways can have a negative effect throughout the regional economy if packages cannot be reliably sent or received. For belly cargo facilities, fast and reliable access to the passenger aircraft apron helps improve on-time performance and therefore customer experience.

In summary, cargo is a riskier proposition for airports, which is possibly why many have not closely engaged with it. Depending on the trajectory of the passenger business after the pandemic, cargo may become a more significant contributor to the bottom line. By better understanding it, airports can add value which then creates new and more diversified revenue streams.

NOTES

1. Air cargo has been traditionally defined as freight and mail. However, data on mail volumes are patchy and it's a business in decline, so when we talk about cargo, we're referring to freight only and use the two terms interchangeably.
2. Air crew, maintenance and insurance.
3. Internationally comparable air freight data are notoriously difficult to obtain, particularly in terms of enplaned-deplaned tonnes at airports, so we use the World Bank's metric of air transport freight of millions of tonne km defined as the volume of freight, express and diplomatic bags carried on each flight stage (operation of an aircraft from take-off to its next landing), measured in tonnes times kilometres travelled.
4. Korean Airlines operates 23 all-cargo aircraft and in 2018 ranks 6th in the world in air freight tonnes kilometres carried: Source: IATA World Air Transport Statistics.
5. R = 0.76.
6. Regressing real US GDP by quarter between Q1 2000 and Q4 2019, so before the pandemic, a 10% change in real GDP translates into a 31% change in air freight but only a 11% change in truck and rail borne cargo.
7. LAX, SFO, YYZ, LHR, CDG, AMS, MUC, SYD, HKG.
8. IATA World Air Transport Statistics.
9. Shirotori and Molina, *South–South Trade*.
10. All data for 2015 from UK Civil Aviation Authority.
11. Bay Area airports comprise San Francisco International (SFO), Oakland International (OAK) and San Jose (SJC).
12. Most airports only require enplaned-deplaned tonnage to be reported, not total cargo processed at on-airport facilities.
13. Defined as Freight Air Transportation (512), Warehousing (521) and Other Postal and Courier Services (532).
14. Defined as the Wythenshawe and Sale East parliamentary constituency. Data from the UK Office of National Statistics.
15. Defined as Northwest Leicestershire parliamentary constituency.
16. Starting in Q1 2011 when e-commerce had 4.7% of the market to Q4 2020 when it had 14.0% is a change of 9.3 which would at the coefficient of 1.12 would add 10.4 points to the air freight index. However, the index increased by 40.7 points over that period, so e-commerce therefore explains about one quarter of the increase in air freight.
17. Cohen and Brown, "Effect of International Airports", 315–335.
18. From 1995 to 2019.
19. From 2009 to 2019.
20. For example, in the first half of 2019, Air France-KLM carried 4.2 million revenue tonne km of cargo and earned 1.1 million euros, a rate of 0.26 euros per revenue tonne km. In the same period, it carried 127,241 million passenger kilometres for which it earned 10,110 million euros for a rate

0.08 euros per passenger kilometre ten human beings, at 100 kg each, is one tonne of humans so the yield is 0.80 euros per "tonne" kilometre or three times more than freight.

21. Correlations between passengers and cargo over the period 2005 to 2019 are 0.83 in Q1, 0.68 in Q2, 0.77 in Q3 and 0.82 in Q4. Data from London Heathrow.
22. Great circle distance.
23. Assumes 2.8 litres per seat per 100 km. Kerosene weighs 0.817 kg per litre.
24. European Aviation Safety Authority.
25. Air cargo is generally measured in tonnes. First, convert that to kilograms by multiplying by 1,000 and then divide that by 100 to get cargo WLUs.
26. Memphis, Tn (FedEx), Louisville, Ky. (UPS) and Anchorage, Ak.
27. The percentage is slightly higher at large airports because integrator operations have probably moved to a secondary airport so above 20 million annual passengers, passengers represent 91% of WLUs.
28. Enplaned-deplaned passenger forecast of 50 million/0.9 equals 55.5 million WLUs of which 5.5 million are cargo and to convert to tonnes multiply by 100 and then divide by 1,000 to get tonnes.
29. A log scale graph shows the *percentage* change in the dependent variable, in this case cargo, relative to a *percentage* change in the independent variable, in this case passengers.
30. Airports Council International-North America, "Air Cargo Guide".
31. A word of caution here: aircraft themselves are generally included in exports by air statistics and because of their high value, they can distort statistics.
32. The only caveat here is that the export of aircraft gets counted as exports but they don't get crated up and shipped by air so the value of air exports may be overstated.
33. Prices from Walmart.ca, May 2021.
34. IATA, "Value of Air Cargo".

Bibliography

Airports Council International-North America. "Air Cargo Guide". Published September 2019. https://airportscouncil.org/wp-content/uploads/2020/03/Air-Cargo-Guide.pdf.

Cohen, Jeffrey P., and Mike Brown. "The Effect of International Airports on Commercial Property Values: Case Studies of Toronto, Ontario, Canada and Vancouver, BC, Canada". *The Economics of Airport Operations (Advances in Airline Economics)* 6 (September 2017): 313–333. https://doi.org/10.1108/S2212-160920170000006012.

European Aviation Safety Authority. "Survey on Standard Weights of Passengers and Baggage". EASA 2008.C.06/30800/R20090095/30800000/FBR/RLO, Zoetermeer, May 2009.

IATA. "Value of Air Cargo: Air Transport and Global Value Chains". Accessed March 9, 2021. https://www.iata.org/en/iata-repository/publications/economic-reports/value-of-air-cargo-air-transport-and-global-value-chains-summary.

Shirotori, Miho, and Ana Cristina Molina. *South–South Trade: The Reality Check. Issues in New Geography of International Trade. United Nations Conference on Trade and Development.* Geneva, United Nations, 2009.

6 AIRPORT AREA PLANNING

INTRODUCTION

In short, airports are magnets which you would expect at the point where international air transport and regional and metropolitan ground transportation networks intersect. It is no surprise, then, that airports and the areas around them have distinct economic characteristics and profound effects on land values beyond their boundaries.[1] Indeed, airports are in some cases emerging as a secondary node of commercial activity in the metropolitan area. While this is nested in the concepts of an Airport City, which can have connotations of a marketing campaign, here we are talking about a more organic concept driven by many individual decisions that proximity to the airport is valuable in a broader sense. For example, the regional economy may be stronger if a company, not aviation related, but reliant on express air freight is allowed to locate on the airport and traditional aviation-related uses that do not need direct access to airside, like fuel storage or car rental service centres, to move off airport. This is a build out of the concept introduced in Chapter 4 of an 'aviation-dependent use' and challenges the binary notion that only aviation-related uses should be permitted within the airport boundary.

AIRPORT AREA CHARACTERISTICS

First, a word about data and definitions. We want to understand the size and composition of economic activity at, and in the vicinity of, airports and for this we will rely on government census data on employment and business establishments. So, our definition of 'airport area' is the airport itself and the immediate vicinity. Here, we encounter a 'trilemma': ideally, we want data that are current, granular geographically and functionally

DOI: 10.4324/9781003173267-6

but, in reality, we can only get two out of three. For example, the geography may not be as fine as we would like but the industry break-down is detailed or vice-versa. The definition of 'airport area' is therefore somewhat elastic. Where we have data by postal code or zip code, we define this area to be the airport itself and the codes that directly about it but in other cases, we must use parliamentary constituencies, census statistical sub-areas or local government areas, which tend to cut a broader swath. We have a reasonable sample of airports around the world but what follows is not intended to be a comprehensive treatment of this topic but rather to present a snapshot of the economic characteristics of the vicinity of airports.

AIRPORT AREA: SIZE

The average share of regional economic activity that the airport area accounts for is 5%, as shown in Figure 6.1. In most cases, this is based on employment but in the case of the US airports, it is calculated by the number of business establishments. The higher shares for London Gatwick (LGW) and Edinburgh (EDI) are partly due to the difficulty in tightly defining the geography of the airport's area. Overall, the data is the most current available, generally from 2018 or 2019.

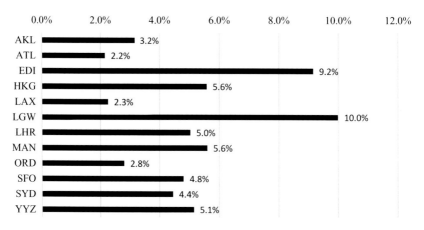

Figure 6.1 Share of Regional Economic Activity in the Airport Area.

Source: Author's calculations from data from the UK Office of National Statistics, US Census, Hong Kong Census, Statistics Canada, Australian Bureau of Statistics, Stats NZ.

AIRPORT AREA: CHARACTERISTICS

If we look at employment patterns at the airport itself and in the area around it and then compare that to the metropolitan area, some important insights emerge. It goes without saying that the airport area will have higher average shares of employment or businesses in transportation, warehousing, accommodation and food services but it's the other sectors that cluster around airports that we are especially interested in.

US

Looking at a sample of 12 major hub US airports,[2] we calculate an 'airport vicinity quotient' (AVQ), shown in Figure 6.2 which is the ratio activity in a particular industry around the airport relative to the region. For example, if manufacturing accounts for 12% of business establishments in the airport area but only 10% in the metropolitan area, the AVQ would be 1.2. When the AVQ is greater than one, that industry is disproportionately located at and around the airport. What we see is that economic activity in manufacturing, wholesale and management of businesses and enterprises[3] and, obviously, transportation and warehousing tend to gravitate towards to the airport. To get the geographical granularity we need, we use numbers of business establishments in each industry as

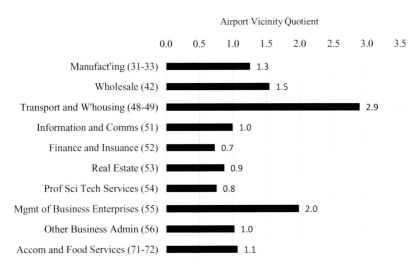

Figure 6.2 Airport Vicinity Quotient: the US.
Source: US Census: County Business Patterns 2018.

opposed to employment, which is suppressed for reasons of commercial confidentiality or unavailable.

The affinity that manufacturing has for the airport area is a result of a few factors. First, airports have historically been in industrial areas, or have caused their vicinity to be so, from the era when the pollution and noise from airport operations were much worse than they are today. Second, the airport vicinity may have been zoned for industrial uses and land is affordable for factories and workshops. Third, some types of manufacturing receive and ship by air and, finally, some airport areas are designated as free trade zones. The same factors probably explain the high AVQ for the wholesale sector and to which we can add access to freeways for distribution. The management of businesses and enterprises has a high AVQ presumably because these enterprises may be geographically far-flung and this sector is more dependent on air transportation than other more locally oriented services such as real estate and finance. These findings are reinforced when we look at the AVQs around major cargo airports in the US[4]; we see higher AVQs for manufacturing and wholesale but a lower AVQ for the management of businesses and enterprises, compared to the major hub airports.

SELECTED GLOBAL HUB AIRPORTS

Looking at a sample of global hub airports,[5] as shown in Figure 6.3, we see that the specialization of economic activity is broadly similar to the US hub sample but in some cases, it is more muted but in another

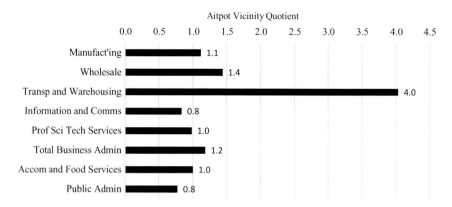

Figure 6.3 Airport Vicinity Quotient: Selected Global Hub Airports.

Source: Author's calculations from data from the UK Office of National Statistics, US Census, Hong Kong Census, Statistics Canada, Australian Bureau of Statistics.

case, it's more pronounced. For example, while the Airport Vicinity Quotient in the US group for Manufacturing is 1.3 and Wholesale is 1.5, it is 1.1 and 1.4, respectively, in the global sample but conversely is also much more specialized in transportation and warehousing. We cannot separate out the Management of Businesses and Enterprises from general Business Administration in the global group but combined it shows a proclivity for locating close to an airport. However, the global hub sample is quite small, so we should consider these results illustrative rather than conclusive particularly since we are blending different methodologies to define the airport area and use employment and business establishments to measure economic activity.[6]

CORRELATIONS

Within each group, there are some notable relationships between the AVQ and the characteristics of the airport. In the global group, the AVQ for total business administration and the degree to which the airport is a passenger airport,[7] and not a freight one, is strongly correlated presumably because of the superior choice of destinations and frequencies. The public administration AVQ is negatively correlated with the share of an airport's revenue from land and property rental. This reflects the fact that most airports have to provide government agencies with space at zero cost for core operations and the public sector's practice of acquiring space through public tender and, as a corollary of that, an aversion to paying premium rents to locate in close proximity to an airport.

In the US group, there were medium to strong correlations between the AVQs for wholesale[8] and manufacturing[9] and the share of international passengers, that is, the more internationally focused an airport is, the greater the degree of clustering of factories and warehouses around it. This speaks to the international nature of supply chains and the additional wide-body belly cargo capacity available at international airports. There is however a negative correlation between the administrative support sector (NAICS 56) and the international share of passengers suggesting that these businesses are primarily domestic focused.

MICRO STUDIES

In this section, we look at some airports and drill down to see how patterns differ between the airport itself and the airport vicinity. While most jurisdictions use NAICS to define industries, some aggregate and disaggregate them in different ways for reporting purposes, for example,

Canada does not report NAICS category 55 separately, which as we saw has a strong affinity for an airport location in the US.

CASE STUDY: TORONTO, CANADA

Unsurprisingly, almost three-quarters of employment at the airport itself is in transportation and warehousing, accommodation and food services and public administration, the latter category picking up all the police offices, border agents and other employees working in public safety and security. What is also noteworthy about Figure 6.4 is that the airport itself has a higher than average share in business services which suggests that aviation-dependent companies are locating as close to the airport as possible.

CASE STUDY: GREAT BRITAIN

Looking at the busiest passenger and cargo airports in Great Britain, and the areas around them,[10] they have higher than average shares of employment in the following industries: transportation and storage, accommodation and food services, information and communications and business administration and support services, as illustrated in Figure 6.5. Information and communications include a wide range of activities from publishing and film production to computer programming and

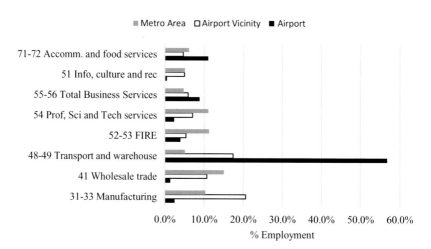

Figure 6.4 Toronto Pearson International Airport Vicinity Characteristics.
Source: Statistics Canada: Census of Canada 2016 and Greater Toronto Airports Authority.

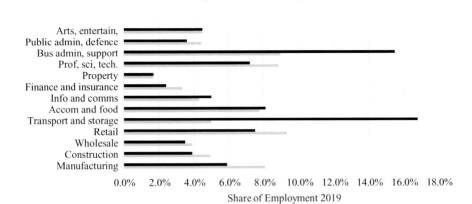

Figure 6.5 Major Airports in Great Britain Employment Characteristics.
Source: UK Office of National Statistics.

consultancy. Given the high propensity for air travel in the IT sector,[11] the clustering of those companies around airports is not surprising. Business administration and support services would include property management, security and investigation, travel booking and tour operators. What differentiates these from professional, scientific and technical services is that they generally involve routine tasks and not complex, technical knowledge.

CASE STUDY: SYDNEY, AUSTRALIA

Around Sydney Airport (SYD), we see the same patterns, shown in Figure 6.6, with the vicinity of the airport[12] having a disproportionately large share of employment in administrative and other support services, finance and real estate but also manufacturing while the airport itself is dominated by employment in the usual suspects of accommodation and food services, transport and warehousing and public administration.

IMPACT ON COMMERCIAL PROPERTY VALUES

Having shown that the area around an airport attracts certain types of industry more than others, this varies by the type of airport, that is, cargo airports tend to attract more manufacturing activity while hub airports

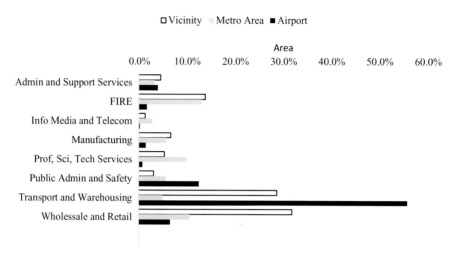

Figure 6.6 Sydney International Airport Vicinity Characteristics.
Source: Australia Bureau of Statistics.

for passengers are attractive to businesses in the field of business administration or head offices. Can we discern how these effects play out in land values around an airport? Yes, we can.

OFFICES

As a general rule, buildings occupied by people (or goods) with high values of time and a high propensity for air travel will pay the largest premium for proximity to an airport.

The value of an office building tends to increase in value by 1.6% every 10% closer it is to the airport, a ratio that appears to be fairly consistent around the world. We know this by looking at large samples of commercial properties around airports and all the factors that drive their value. This includes the type of building, for example, office versus warehouse, building age, size and quality, that is, Class A versus Class B or C office space, neighbourhood characteristics, access to public transport, proximity to the CBD and to the airport. We then run a regression analysis on this which tells us, how a property's value is affected by distance or travel time to the airport,[13] if at all, while controlling for all the other factors. Proximity to an airport is generally a significant factor in explaining a commercial property's value but usually only a small one compared to, for example, the size of the property because that ultimately determines the revenue stream.

We also looked at the role of office size and found that proximity to the airport, as a general rule, is more valuable to large offices because there are more employees and the aggregate travel costs in time and money are greater.

If traffic congestion is chronic or access to the airport requires going through a potential bottleneck such as a tunnel or bridge, this value gradient gets steeper. Investments in faster, more reliable ground access, for example, a rail link, flattens the gradient which means that properties further away become more valuable.

The implication for airports is that investing in faster and/or more reliable ground access boosts office values throughout the region. Suppose there is an office building 20 km from the airport that is worth $10 million but driving to the airport is the only viable option and the trip can be long and unreliable. The airport invests in a rail line and the value of the office building now increases by the difference between the old, steep traffic-congested gradient and the new, shallower rail-based one. However, the airport sees none of that value uplift but the owner and the governments that levy taxes based on value certainly do. Is it unreasonable to suggest that the airport should see some of that value-add credited to its own tax bill? Conceptually, this is illustrated in Figure 6.7.

. . . .

Case Studies

LONDON, ENGLAND

Based on a sample of approximately 10% of the 15,000 or so office premises in Greater London and valuations in 2015, the analysis shows that while the main driver of an office building's value is its floor area and location relative to Central London, it's also affected by ease of access to London Heathrow Airport (LHR).

Because London is a large, very congested city, we looked not only at road distance to the airport but also travel times by car and public transport.

Driving time gradients are steeper than for driving distances which is what we would expect: valuation is more sensitive to travel times, which is what people actually experience, than a fixed road distance. So, an office building close to LHR but connected to it by chronically congested roads may be worth less than one further away but with a shorter and/or more reliable travel time to the airport.

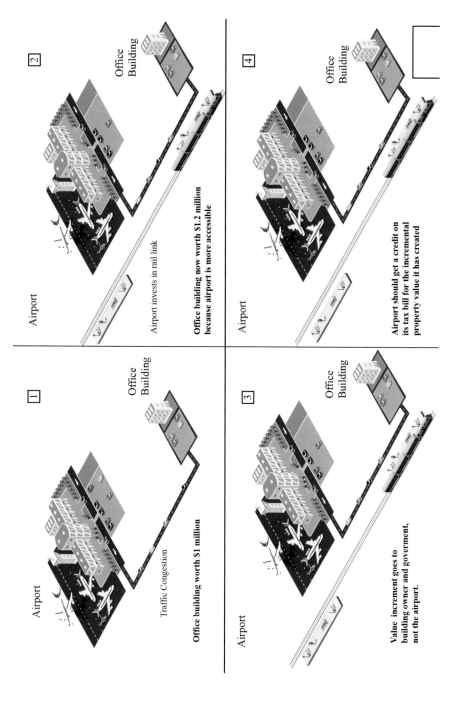

Figure 6.7 Impact of Ground Access Improvements on Commercial Property Values.

Where ground access time is long and/or unreliable, the travel time gradient is steeper. For example, offices located south of the River Thames that require a bridge crossing, potentially a bottleneck, to get to LHR, have a driving time gradient steeper than average, as shown in Figure 6.8. Please note that the gradients show the impact on value of proximity to the airport holding other factors that drive value such as building age, quality and location relative to the CBD constant. In other words, offices in Mayfair and the West End are worth more than in Hounslow and Hammersmith but the chart below is just showing the airport proximity component of overall office valuation.

Public transport's influence is highly significant. Travel time gradients for trips by public transport are shallower because rail trips are, if not always faster, generally more reliable … and productive if you have a seat and table. Picture two identical office buildings, both 20 km from LHR, the one by a train station will be worth more, as shown in Figure 6.9.

TORONTO, CANADA

Toronto Pearson International Airport (YYZ) handled 50 million passengers in 2019, serving a metropolitan area of 6 million people.

This was a longitudinal study using sales prices. The sample included 471 commercial properties around Toronto Pearson that sold between the years 2000 and 2015. Commercial properties are

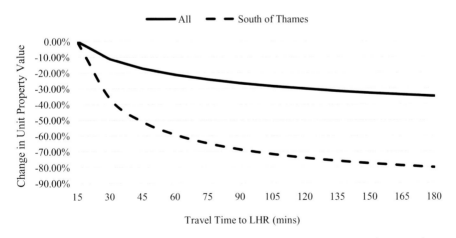

Figure 6.8 Office Value Gradients: Impact of Traffic Congestion London Heathrow Airport.

Source: Author's calculations from UK Value Office Agency and Google Maps data.

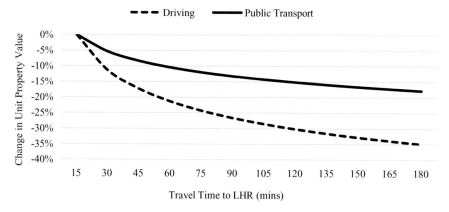

Figure 6.9 Office Value Gradients: Impact of Public Transport London Heathrow Airport.

Source: Author's calculations from UK Value Office Agency and Google Maps data.

defined as office buildings and hotels. Driving distance is defined as the shortest driving distance between the property and the airport passenger terminal on Google Maps. Real sales costs were used, that is, adjusted for inflation, so any valuation increase was not just down to general price increases.

In summary, we found that lot size, the number of international flights (as proxy for air network connectivity), driving distance to the airport and certain neighbourhood effects explain 55% of the variation in real commercial property sales prices around Toronto Pearson Airport between 2000 and 2015.

Specifically, a 10% increase in international flights at Toronto Pearson Airport, as a proxy measure for connectivity, translated into a 6.9% increase in commercial property values and every 10% further away from Toronto Pearson by road, a commercial property is worth 1.6% less, all other things equal.

Unsurprisingly, hotel valuations were more sensitive to international connectivity and proximity to airport than offices. Every 10% increase in international flights increased a hotel's value by 22% and every 10% further away from the airport, its value declines by 2.5%. In other words, the distance gradient is steeper. Why is this? When you consider the amount of shuttling back and forth by flight crew and passengers on any given day, and the high value of time those people likely have, the shorter the distance, a hotel can fill more rooms, command higher rates and incurs lower shuttle bus costs. Figure 6.3 earlier showed the clustering of hotels at Toronto Pearson for this reason.

Just by being situated in certain neighbourhoods increases and decreases value, for example, a building in a manicured business park commands a higher price than one in a run-down, industrial area by virtue of that alone.

SYDNEY, AUSTRALIA

For this analysis, we used a sample of just over 400 commercial premises in Greater Sydney, as recorded by the New South Wales (NSW) Valuer General's Office (VGO). Only land values are available.

As in other cities, we found that the main driver of the value of commercial land in Greater Sydney is the area of the parcel and other property and neighbourhood characteristics. However, proximity to Sydney Airport (SYD) is a small but significant factor. Land value declines by 1.6% every 10% further by road the premises are from the airport. In rank order of the importance of proximity to SYD, the top three land use categories are B3 Commercial Core, B7 Business Parks and B5 Business Development, suggesting that these zones accommodate uses with a higher propensity for air travel and higher values of time. Mixed use developments have a lower affinity for airport proximity presumably because they have a residential component.

The importance of proximity to SYD appears to be directly related to ease of ground access. Land values in the south west part of Greater Sydney decline at a lower rate with respect to distance from the airport because this area can be reached by a tolled motorway or direct train service. By contrast, access from the western part of Greater Sydney, for example, Parramatta and Blacktown, is more challenging, so land values decline more steeply with distance from SYD. This represents an obvious business opportunity for the new Western Sydney Airport (WSA) which we discussed in Chapter 2.

VANCOUVER, CANADA

Vancouver International Airport (YVR) processed about 25 million passengers in 2019 and serves a metropolitan area of 2.5 million people.

The original Vancouver study, the first of its type, was conducted in 2013 and using a sample of just under 2,200 business premises in the City of Richmond, the host municipality to YVR. We combined business licence and property value data sets to see how proximity to the airport varied between industries and found very different distance gradients. As in Toronto, this is most important for hotels which declined by 6.5% in value every 10% further away from YVR. The next steepest gradient was corporate head offices, which occupied buildings that declined in value at a rate of 6.4% because the occupants have a high propensity for air travel and high values of time. This reflects the findings from the sample of US airports discussed earlier where the management of businesses and enterprises show a strong affinity for the airport area. Manufacturing reported a 4.3% distance gradient probably because manufacturers receive and dispatch high value-to-weight parts and products by air.

Locally focused businesses such as health care, finance and insurance, food and retail either had low distance gradients or positive ones, that is, the buildings they occupy became more valuable the further away from the airport.

MANCHESTER, ENGLAND

Greater Manchester is a metropolitan area in North West England with a population of 2.8 million and is the second most populous built-up area in the UK after London. Manchester Airport (MAN) is one of the UK's busiest airports serving 28.3 million passengers in 2018.

We found very similar results to LHR, that is, travel time is more important than distance as is congestion en route. The main drivers of the value of offices premises in Greater Manchester are the area and other property and neighbourhood characteristics but proximity to the airport is a small but significant factor. For example, the value of an office in Greater Manchester declines by 1.8% every 10% further by road it is from the airport, 2.4% less every 10% further in terms of driving time but only 1.4% less every 10% further in terms of public transport time. Figure 6.10

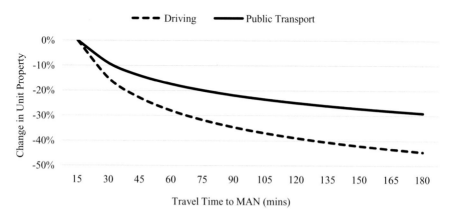

Figure 6.10 Office Value Gradients: Impact of Public Transport Manchester Airport.

Source: Author's calculations from UK Value Office Agency and Google Maps data.

shows, first, the travel time gradients for an identical building in every respect except travel time to Manchester Airport. So, we are controlling for all the other drivers of property value such as building quality, age and condition and neighbourhood amenities to isolate the role of proximity to the airport, in this case, measured in travel time.

The driving time gradient is slightly steeper than public transport closer in possibly because of traffic congestion around the airport. Second, the further away from the airport, the value gap grows because the premium that gets capitalized into property value for reliable travel times increases.

REGIONAL AIRPORTS IN SOUTHERN ONTARIO

Turning to smaller airports, we looked at the 1,615 commercial and industrial property sales around the eight airports in Southern Ontario that occurred between 2011 and 2017 and we find that the value of the property declines by 1.7% for every 10% further it is from the airport, so, take two identical buildings and the one that is 10% further away from the airport will, by that fact alone, be worth 1.7% less.

When we look at office buildings, the distance gradient is even higher: these properties are worth 4.9% less every 10% further away from the airport they're located. For warehouse properties, the distance gradient is much lower at 2.6% decline in value for every 10% further from the airport.

The explanation for this difference may partly be that average wages in industries likely to occupy offices are higher than in those likely to occupy warehouses, so the value of time is higher. For example, in 2017, the average hourly wages in Ontario in manufacturing and transportation and warehousing were approximately 30% lower than in finance, real estate and professional and technical services.

WAREHOUSES

A class of real estate very much in the news during the Covid-19 pandemic has been big distribution warehouses (BDWs). How are the values of BDWs affected by proximity to an airport?

We look at England's two largest cargo airports, London Heathrow (LHR) and East Midlands Airport (EMA). The former is a global passenger hub while the latter is more of an industrial airport, located close to the geographic centre of the English population.

Proximity to an airport with cargo services has a small but significant impact on the value of a Big Distribution Warehouse (BDW) in England. The impact is seen most in BDWs with a national or international focus.

The main driver of the value of a BDW is its area and specialized fixtures and fittings to support retail or post and courier operations, for example, refrigeration or sorting machinery.

Proximity to LHR is likely valued more highly than to EMA because of the scale of LHR's cargo ecosystem and the range of air connections on offer. The greater density of road traffic around LHR also increases the value of proximity. In the case of EMA, the value of a BDW is most sensitive to driving time which would be expected given the concentration of 'just-in-time' all-cargo and courier airlines at EMA.

A final important finding is that there are clusters of BDW's in England and being in one increases the value of an individual BDW due to the presence of specialty suppliers and access to skilled labour pools.

RESIDENTIAL

The reality is that aircraft create noise that annoys people even though planes have become quieter. Meanwhile, air traffic control is becoming more precise, for example, a continuous approach descent means that engine thrust as the plane levels off on its way down is eliminated. As a result, despite an increase in the number of aircraft movements, the overall noise footprint for many airports has shrunk.

This is not the place to get into a technical discussion of the different ways of measuring aircraft noise, or how aircraft noise affects people's health, well-being and residential property values except to say that these are complex issues on which extensive research has been undertaken, including a study of housing prices around Atlanta International Airport (ATL), the world's busiest.[14] The analysis found that houses in neighbourhoods more affected by aircraft noise did sell for less, all other things equal, but this effect was mitigated because overall proximity to the airport is correlated with higher housing prices which are also buoyed by a metropolitan area that is more prosperous because it is well connected by air.

In many jurisdictions, it is a regulatory requirement to produce noise contours based on future demand and operating conditions with best practice being to run a series of scenarios based on potential runway operating patterns, aircraft fleet mixes, stage lengths and day and night operations.

Most airports err on the side of caution when drawing noise contours, that is, they tend to protect a greater area than may be necessary but given the uncertainties around future levels and patterns of aircraft movements, no medals are handed out for taking land out of the contour if residents will be adversely affected by noise. It is entirely rational and prudent for airports to do this, but in the spirit of 'beyond the boundaries', this could freeze land that would otherwise be available for residential development and, in cities with housing price affordability challenges, exacerbate that problem.

Why should an airport care about housing affordability? At a strategic level, it may make the region uncompetitive in attracting investment, jobs and students. It may force airport workers, particularly low paid ones, into longer commutes or crowded dwellings which the pandemic has shown is a major risk in the spread of Covid-19.

It also depresses the demand for air travel. Controlling for after-tax household income and the average value of the dwelling, to capture the wealth effect, a 10% increase in share of 'shelter-stressed' owners, that is, those spending more than 30% of their income on housing, in Vancouver depresses spending on airline tickets by 1.6%. The comparable number in Toronto is −0.8%.

It's a long series of linkages, and it may not work in all cases, but the argument is that overly broad Noise Exposure Forecast (NEF) contours may constrain housing supply, which exacerbates housing affordability issues which then presents problems for workforce attraction and retention, both regionally and at the airport and ultimately there is less money in the household's budget for air travel.

Many people want to live near the airport. In every major Canadian metropolitan area, households that spend more on airline tickets live closer to the airport, as shown for three cities in Figure 6.11. While many factors explain why a household lives where it does, a 10% increase in distance from the airport translates into between a 0.5% and 1.0% reduction in spending on airline tickets.

Another observation is that when we look at affluent neighbourhoods, as shown in Table 6.1, in a selection of global cities they are on average 30 minutes' drive away from the airport reflecting the value of the residents' time and frequency of trips to the airport.

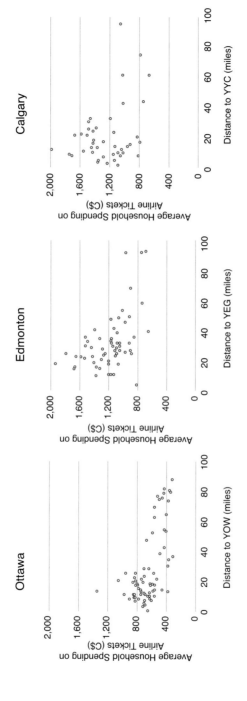

Figure 6.11 Household Spending on Airline Tickets and Distance to Airport Ottawa, Edmonton and Calgary Airports.

Source: Statistics Canada, Survey of Household Spending, 2017 and author's analysis.

Note: Each dot is a postal code.

Table 6.1 Affluent Neighbourhoods and Proximity to Airports

Metro Area	Neighbourhood with the Highest Income	Driving Distance to Airport (km)	Driving Time to Airport (mins)
Amsterdam	Oud Zuid	14.3	17
Hong Kong	The Peak	45.6	46
London	Westminster	24.0	36
Los Angeles	Beverly Glen	17.6	25
Munich	Schwabing West	31.8	32
Paris	16e Arrondissement	33.7	39
San Francisco	South Beach-Yerba Buena	22.0	19
Sydney	Double Bay	14.6	21
Toronto	Moore Park	24.6	35
Average		25.4	30

Source: Various Governments Census Data, Google Maps.

INTEGRATED PLANNING

This sounds like one of those motherhood statements that we all genuflect to but is maddeningly vague. Who could possibly argue that integrated planning isn't better than the disintegrated variety? In this case, the payoff is financial, which tends to be motivator, as both the airport and surrounding areas will be better off.

This chapter has illustrated the potential for win-win outcomes, for example, if adjacent municipalities understand airports' positive effect on commercial property values, sufficient land and density can be permitted to take full advantage. Likewise, airports can loosen overly conservative NEF contours, free up land for residential development and help make housing more affordable.

An example of disintegrated planning is when an airport plans a retail mall targeted at the local market because it has some orphaned land or can offer developers incentives and exemptions from local planning rules. These tend to be zero sum outcomes that often backfire on the airport strategically and operationally. It can sour the long-term relationship between airport and host municipality while some airports have been forced to make public service announcements advising passengers to plan for longer ground access times because of traffic congestion, before Christmas, at the retail mall that the airport itself permitted!

It's accepted that the planning cycles of the airport and jurisdictions beyond the boundary are rarely synchronized which makes integrated planning challenging but not impossible.

SUMMARY AND CONCLUSIONS

A CEO could be forgiven if he or she believes that their airport is a blight on the surrounding community, based on complaints from residents over aircraft noise or vehicle traffic and from local politicians about its allegedly meagre contribution to municipal finances.

In fact, the opposite is true; airports tend to increase the value of commercial property around them, and house prices are generally positively correlated with proximity to the airport. This phenomenon is not confined to large, hub airports either.

The exact mix of industries and land-uses around an airport depends on many things, not least the type of airport so those focused on cargo, or international gateways, are more likely to attract manufacturing uses than a domestic hub. This harks back to the importance of strategic clarity about the markets the airport intends to pursue and prosper in.

Of course, it has been ever thus. Research into commercial rents in medieval Gloucester, England found that there was a premium commanded at the High Cross, where several arterial roads converged.[15]

About 5% of a region's economic activity in the vicinity of the major airport and tends to attract industries with a higher propensity to use passenger and freight air transportation, for example, manufacturing, wholesale, management of business enterprises and, of course, transportation and warehousing.

Host municipalities can reap more tax dollars and deliver better services at a lower burden to residents because of the airport, a fact that frequently gets overlooked in the negotiations about the appropriate contribution.

If a rail link is built to the airport, there is a further value uplift, as the benefits of faster and more reliable access get capitalized into office values. None of this increment is typically captured by the airport that may have funded all or part of the rail connection. There are ways of doing so, without the airport buying these properties but undeniably there are theoretical and practical challenges. A reasonable first step is to calculate what the uplift is and at least have it credited to the airport's economic impact account.

Some residential property values are depressed because of aircraft noise but there are many ways to mitigate this from insulation to financial compensation. In general, though, households with a high propensity for air travel tend to live closer to the airport and the most affluent neighbourhoods tend to be 30-minute drive away. On a broader scale, house prices benefit from the prosperity delivered to the region by a well-connected airport.

Integrated planning of the airport area reduces the risk of municipalities undersupplying commercial land and density or airports sterilizing land for residential development that could make housing more affordable by clinging to outdated noise contours.

The traditional approach of only allowing aviation-related uses at the airport may impair the regional economy by denying an aviation-dependent company a proximate location to maximize its productivity and competitiveness while some aviation-related businesses can be more widely dispersed.

NOTES

1. This chapter does not deal with obstacle limitation zoning in this chapter, that is, regulations that prevent a tall building 'puncturing' the approach or take-off surfaces because it is a highly technical matter and best dealt with elsewhere.
2. We focus on US airports because we can assemble a reasonable sample with the consistency of US Census data.
3. NAICS (North American Industry Classification System) code 55 is defined as the Management of Companies and Enterprises sector as comprising: (1) establishments that hold the securities of (or other equity interests in) companies and enterprises for the purpose of owning a controlling interest or influencing management decisions or (2) establishments (except government establishments) that administer, oversee and manage establishments of the company or enterprise and that normally undertake the strategic or organizational planning and decision making role of the company or enterprise. Establishments that administer, oversee and manage may hold the securities of the company or enterprise. Establishments in this sector perform essential activities that are often undertaken, in-house, by establishments in many sectors of the economy. By consolidating the performance of these activities of the enterprise at one establishment, economies of scale are achieved.
4. Memphis (MEM), Louisville (SDF), Oakland (OAK) and Indianapolis (IND).
5. Hong Kong (HKG), London Heathrow (LHR), Los Angeles (LAX), San Francisco (SFO), Sydney (SYD) and Toronto (YYZ).
6. For the two US airports in the Global Hub group, business establishments by industry are used to calculate the AVQ while for the other airports, it is employment.

7. Measured as the share of total Workload Units (WLUs) accounted for by passengers.
8. R = 0.51.
9. R = 0.69.
10. Defined as the parliamentary constituency in which the airport is located.
11. Based on US data for 2019, this sector spends about $2,024 per employee on air travel per year compared to a service sector average of $999.
12. Defined as Australian Bureau of Statistics areas: Mascot-Eastlakes, Botany, Tempe-St Peters, Arncliffe, Monterey-Brighton-le-Sands. All these statistical areas abut Sydney Airport which is its own statistical area.
13. We measure travel distances and times using Google Maps.
14. Cohen and Coughlin, "Changing Noise Levels", 287–313.
15. Casson and Casson, "Location, Location, Location", 575–599.

BIBLIOGRAPHY

Casson, Catherine, and Mark Casson. "Location, Location, Location? Analysing Property Rents in Medieval Gloucester". *Economic History Review* 69, no. 2 (May 2016): 575–599. https://doi.org/10.1111/ehr.12117.

Cohen, Jeffrey P., and Cletus C. Coughlin. "Changing Noise Levels and Housing Prices Near the Atlanta Airport". *Growth and Change* 40, no. 2 (June 2009): 287–313. https://doi.org/10.1111/j.1468-2257.2009.00476.x.

7

ECONOMIC IMPACT

INTRODUCTION

We noted in Chapter 1 that a key objective of strategic planning is maintaining and building social licence. One way to do this is by measuring airports' roles as economic engines in their own right and as enablers of wider economic activity.

Allowing for some differences in definitions and timing, the correlation between airport size and economic impact is a strong one,[1] as Figure 7.1 shows. The rule of thumb here is that each million enplaned-depleaned passengers results in 1,000 direct jobs or, putting it another way, every 1,000 passengers supports one job at an airport.

International passengers tend to create more jobs per capita because of customs and immigration, a greater propensity to check bags and access to duty free shopping.

TRADITIONAL APPROACH

A traditional economic impact assessment will count the jobs at the airport and, based on that, the taxes and value added to the economy. Jobs are subdivided into direct, indirect and induced categories and the way to think about this is:

- the direct job is the person fuelling the aircraft,
- the indirect job is the person working in a garage off the airport fixing the fuel truck, and
- the induced job is the person serving at a local restaurant because the first two have paycheques.

DOI: 10.4324/9781003173267-7

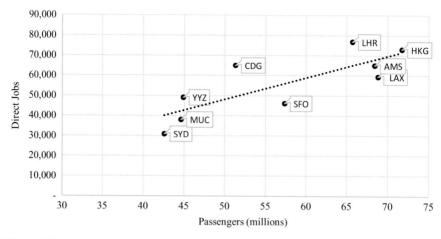

Figure 7.1 Airport Size and Economic Impact.
Source: Various Airports' Economic Impact Studies.

In practical terms, the process starts with the airport sending a survey or to all the businesses and organizations working at the airport, asking for information on number of direct employees and status, full-time or part-time and payroll. Think of this as the census. Companies should also be asked to include contract staff performing core tasks, for example, if IT is outsourced.

While every airport will have an official list of tenants and other business partners, a Google search of addresses on airport property, particularly multi-tenant buildings will reveal several 'hidden' companies operating and they should be included in the survey too.

For various reasons, the response rate to such surveys has been declining, so other methods need to be deployed. Police and security agencies are particularly reluctant to divulge numbers for understandable reasons. Employee parking pass data can give a sense of how many employees work for a company and wages can be estimated from regional averages for those businesses. For jobs in parking and ground transportation, employment estimates can be arrived at by multiplying the number and duration of taxi and TNC trips to and from the airport based on surveys of ground access mode choice.[2] A final resort can be to visit the premises and count the cars parked outside. In other words, a certain amount of ingenuity is required. Of course, employment numbers or payroll at individual companies should never be disclosed publicly but they can be rolled up into categories such as 'air carrier' or 'retail'.

Most direct jobs will be located on the airport but not all of them. For example, staff selling tickets for the airport rail line in the CBD can be considered directly employed associated with on-going operation of the airport. We can include hotel staff around the airport, at least in proportion to the business the hotel derives from the airport.[3]

The factors that convert direct jobs into indirect and induced ones are known as multipliers and come from macro-economic models of the economy known as an Input-Output (IO) model. It's unlikely that airports have the skills in-house or access to one, so this is where consultants come into the picture. However, many jurisdictions publish multipliers in the form of look-up tables which can be applied to the survey results if they're looking for a fast and cheap economic impact assessment.

Confusion tends to abound over the jobs number. First, some airports broadcast the total direct, indirect and induced number[4] while others stick to direct jobs. The advantage of the latter number is that it's real, tangible and a simple answer to a frequently asked question: 'how many people work at the airport?'. The indirect and induced jobs are outputs from the model. Second, the model will produce employment numbers in terms of jobs and person years (PYs). The number of jobs will always be higher than the PYs because of part-time employment, for example, one full-time job and one part-time job equals two jobs but only 1.5 PYs. It is technically more accurate to report PYs but that term is alien to most of the audience whereas everybody knows what a job is. Over time there will be a job number and a PY number out there which ends confusing everybody. Better to stick with one number, direct jobs, with the footnote that some of them are part-time and that there's a raft of other related jobs around the airport.

In additional to taxes generated by employment, taxes should also include any value-added taxes on airline tickets,[5] security fees, retail, food and beverage sales and ground access trips.

Applying a geographical lens is important too as the number of jobs in each part of the region will be of interest to elected officials as well as in planning ground access infrastructure and services.[6] Security badge and employee parking permit data bases, stripped of individuals' names and other personal details, can be used to calculate the number of employees residing in each postcode, for example.[7]

Traditional economic impact assessments have their challenges.

Substantively

- Some airports, for example, Munich (MUC) present a consolidated report of its economic, social and environmental impact reflecting a commitment to sustainability.
- Consolidation, automation and downsizing has resulted in the number of direct jobs stagnating or declining. For example, between 2005 and 2010, Vancouver International Airport (YVR) saw a 9.2% decrease in direct employment despite a 2.5% increase in passengers.
- The focus is on the quantity of jobs, not the quality which is a problem given the contemporary issues around about income inequality, job security and a minimum living wage. In other words, not all jobs are created equal.
- Reluctance of business partners and other organizations to participate due to changes in corporate data policy, loss of autonomy by local managers and a 'do more with less' culture.

Presentationally:

- Some economic impact assessments stretch incredulity, so the audience has become sceptical.
- The message gets lost in the noise. Every organization, project or cause seems to have an economic impact assessment which tells elected officials there will be this many jobs, that much tax revenue and value added to the economy if you support it.
- The numbers blur: a billion dollars here, a million dollars there, we are inundated with statistics but often without any context. Much better to say something like: 'the taxes generated by the airport pay for the local hospital to operate for five days'. For example, an economic impact assessment of a small airport in northern British Columbia, Canada concluded that the federal taxes generated paid for the annual operating costs of the town's RCMP detachment[8] Factoids or soundbites that resonate are key.
- Written reports tend to gather dust on a shelf so rendering the information in a visually compelling way, for example, by video or infographics is important.

Finally, they can be expensive, costing $100,000 and up.

Many of these challenges can be overcome but it would be reasonable to say that a traditional impact assessment is a necessary but not sufficient condition to communicate the true economic significance of an airport.

TARGETED IMPACTS

In many cases, an airport will be interested in its economic impact on particular groups, for example, women, young people or disadvantaged neighbourhoods.

CASE STUDY: BERMUDA AIRPORT REDEVELOPMENT

The Government of Bermuda was particularly interested in the impact on employment amongst certain targeted groups of a $1.9 billion expansion of the terminal building at Bermuda Airport (BDA). Construction has an impact on female employment: a 10% increase in construction GDP results in a 0.7% increase in female employment, one year later, either as construction paycheques find their way into businesses that employ more females or females replace males who have taken construction jobs.

In terms of on-going operations, Table 7.1 shows that the airport is particularly important for youth employment.

CASE STUDY: TORONTO'S LOW-INCOME NEIGHBOURHOODS

The propensity to work[9] at Pearson International Airport in low-income neighbourhoods in Toronto[10] is 20% higher than the city average, after controlling for other factors, including commuting distance. Training opportunities and apprenticeship programs could be directed at schools in these areas, for example.

CONSTRUCTION IMPACTS

Because capital projects are lumpy and sporadic, the convention is to include only jobs associated with the on-going operation of the airport

Table 7.1 Bermuda Airport (BDA) Targeted Economic Impacts

Target Group	A 10% Increase in Passengers Results in This % Change in Employment
Bermudians	0.6
Females	1.8
Youth	7.1

in the traditional economic impact assessment, but a separate one can be undertaken for construction projects.

Many jurisdictions have 'look-up' tables by which the jobs, tax and GDP impacts of construction can easily be estimated, recognizing that they will be average figures. For example, building a runway will likely have different impacts to an office building because of the distinct nature of the inputs, materials and skill sets required. The larger and more specialized the project, the greater the likelihood that the airport will want to commission a customized assessment.

The potency of these assessments can be increased by focusing on broader outcomes or on targeted groups, for example, in terms of building human capital, a 10% increase in investment in building structures in British Columbia (BC), Canada, leads to a 3.5% increase in people registered in apprenticeship programs in the construction trades in BC while every 10% increase in the value of building permits in BC, increases the aboriginal employment rate by 1.8%.

CATALYTIC IMPACTS

When we refer to catalytic economic impacts, we are talking about how an airport and the connectivity it provides stimulates goods exports, tourism, international education and inward investment. While these can and should be quantified, the real power comes from the narratives.

Exports are goods and services consumed by non-residents which adds to the size of the economy, allows domestic companies to reap economies of scale, as well as being exposed to more competition, stimulating further efficiencies and innovation. Most people associate exports with tangible items like machine parts or foodstuffs but a tourist, international student or investor is an export too. Basically, any time a non-resident buys or consumes something in or from your country, that's an export.

THE BC CHERRY STORY

The Okanagan Valley in central British Columbia, Canada has a semi-desert climate, making it home to some of Canada's premier vineyards and orchards. One of the fruits grown there are cherries and as the summer progresses, the growing season moves north and the Okanagan cherries ripen just in time for September and Harvest Festival in China,

Taiwan and Hong Kong where they are considered delicacies. The daily cycle is that cherries are picked in the morning before the hottest part of the day, packed and dispatched by truck to Vancouver International Airport (YVR) 400 km away where they are loaded onto one of the late night/early morning flights to Asia. The elapsed time from a cherry being plucked from a tree in the Okanagan Valley to being in somebody's breakfast cereal in Hong Kong is 36 hours. Except when things go wrong like the longer, south runway at YVR is out of service due to maintenance and only the shorter north runway is available. Because air carriers are understandably reluctant to ask passengers to get off the plane to lighten the load, it's the BC cherries that get left behind on a warm summer night. The ground crew just want to go home, the overtime budget is exhausted or just not knowing any better, the cherries end up rotting on the apron. When Vancouver Airport Authority started to talk about lengthening the north runway, it did so in terms of removing a constraint in the distribution channel for a key BC export. Rita McGrath is a professor at Columbia Business School and her strategic admonition[11] is that 'snow melts from the edges', so the diligent airport CEO takes a morning drive around the ramp every now and then to see what cargo has been left behind.

THE AUSSIE SKIER STORY

Another narrative from British Columbia, Canada concerns Australians coming up for the world-class skiing at Whistler/Blackcomb and resorts in the Interior such as Sun Peaks in Kamloops, BC, and Big White at Kelowna, BC.

The complete package includes a week of great skiing with a side trip to see a Kamloops Blazers hockey game and sample the local craft beers and wines. Despite all this, it's undeniably a long way to travel. As we saw in Chapter 3, the advent of non-stop flights across the Pacific hurt Honolulu Airport (HNL) but it has helped the end points. What was a 21-hour flight between Sydney and Vancouver via Hawaii now takes approximately 15 hours, so more Australians are visiting BC. We only have a short time series but it suggests that every 10% increase in direct flights has led to a 4.3% increase in visitors from Down Under, as shown in Figure 7.2.

After such a long time cooped up on a plane, these generally very affluent visitors want to get on the slopes as soon as possible. That assumes that their skis, poles and boots arrive at the same time but the turboprop aircraft, generally a Dash-8 or Q-400, that fly them up from Vancouver

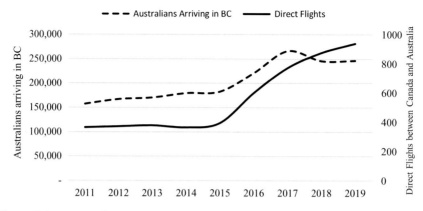

Figure 7.2 Impact of Direct Flights on Tourism.

do not always have the baggage capacity to carry all the equipment. Big White Resort and Kelowna Airport (YLW) were encouraged when United Airlines flew a regional jet to LAX providing a higher capacity air access option.

THE ROBOT REPAIR CREW STORY

In a drab industrial estate in Barrie, Ontario, about one hour's drive north of Toronto, sits the headquarters of a company called Innovative Automation (IA), a global leader in automating production lines and other processes. With customers around the world, staring at millions of dollars in losses when a line is shut down even for a day, IA must dispatch repair crews at short notice to fix the malfunctioning robot. The fact that there is daily or double daily service to most parts of the world available at Toronto Pearson International Airport (YYZ) makes this possible and for IA to employ more people, win export awards and fund bursaries at local colleges.

HUB AIRPORTS AND AIR CARRIERS AS EXPORTERS

A final angle that has not been explored is that while we have talked about airports as enablers of exports of goods and services, what about the air transport sector itself? When a hub airport and its major carrier work together to entice non-residents to travel on and through them, that's an export. Simply put, every resident of India that buys a ticket on Emirates Airlines and connects through Dubai (DXB) is counted as an export of the UAE.

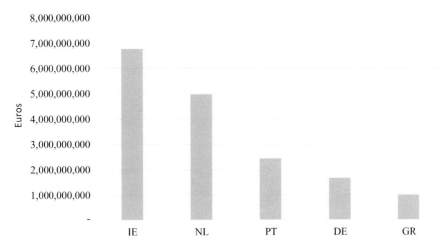

Figure 7.3 Net Exports of Air Transport Services.
Source: IMF.

Looking at Europe, the top five net exporters of air transport services[12] are shown in Figure 7.3.

Ireland earns more money, net, from air transport than any other country in Europe because it is the domicile of Ryanair and home to some of the world's largest aircraft leasing companies while Aer Lingus and Dublin Airport (DUB) have established themselves as a secondary gateway to Europe. Netherlands is second because of Schiphol Airport (AMS) and KLM. Portugal ranks highly because Lisbon Airport (LIS) and the airline TAP operate a gateway to Brazil, Germany because of Lufthansa's global hubs at FRA and MUC and finally Greece, possibly from flying tourists around the islands.

Meanwhile, Canadians have become steadily more dependent on foreign air carriers. Figure 7.4 shows the balance of payments in this sector over the last approximately 20 years with Canadians buying more tickets on foreign air carriers than foreigners are buying from Canadian air carriers.

GEOGRAPHY OF ECONOMIC IMPACTS

Most airport economic impact studies enumerate the numbers at a regional or metropolitan level, that is, broadly consistent with the catchment area; however, it is possible to use a larger or a smaller geographical canvas.

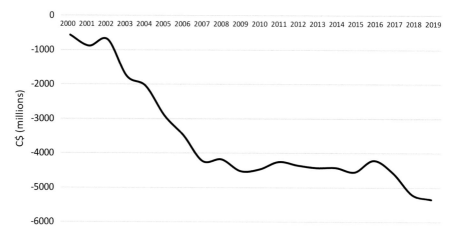

Figure 7.4 Canada's Balance of Payments in Air Passenger Transport Services.

Source: Statistics Canada. Table 36-10-0005-01 International transactions in services, transportation by category, annual.

NATIONAL IMPACTS

Larger airports will have national economic impacts. As a case study, Toronto Pearson International Airport (YYZ) enables economic activity in every province and territory of Canada. For example, agricultural scientists in Saskatchewan travel to meet partners in India. It is estimated that 65% of the world's lentils are grown in Saskatchewan, and India is a key market. Diamonds mined in the Northwest Territories are sent to Antwerp, Belgium for cutting while tourists from Japan visit 'Anne of Green Gables' in Prince Edward Island. They all connect through Toronto Pearson which can be presented in a visually compelling manner, an example of which can be found at www.greatairports.ca.

LOCAL IMPACTS

Ultimately what an airport needs is a localized measure of its impact, or relevance, that speaks to politicians where it hits closest to home, namely, their electoral prospects in the district they represent. As Tip O'Neill, former Speaker of the US House of Representatives memorably said: 'all politics is local'.

Elected officials will hear the aggregate numbers, for example, that the airport supports 49,000 direct jobs but ask 'what does that mean for me'? So, we introduce the concept of the Airport Relevance Index (ARI) to illustrate the local impacts.[13]

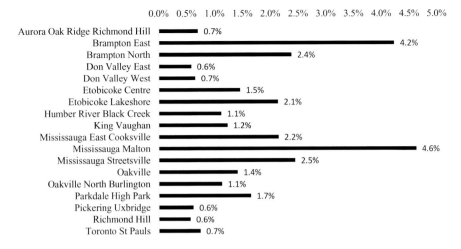

Figure 7.5 Local Economic Impacts: Airport Employment.
Source: Greater Toronto Airports Authority, Statistics Canada, Author.

As Figure 7.5 shows, the Members of Parliament for Brampton East and Mississauga Malton, two federal election districts close to Toronto Pearson, will be keenly interested in the airport's health and well-being.

The conversation with the elected representatives for Don Valley West and Toronto St Paul's will be different and focused on the strong appetite their voters display for air travel, as shown in Figure 7.6, as opposed to the percentage that work at Toronto Pearson. For example, policy changes that would allow more non-stop air service and a greater choice of air carriers would resonate with these politicians.

The conversation with MPs in another set of ridings would centre around business travel. Most airports will have a ground access survey which should have data on the geographic origin of the trip to the airport and its purpose. Usually, the starting point of a trip is an address or post-code which can then be geocoded to a riding and then cross-referenced by trip purpose. So, what we are capturing, as shown in Figure 7.7, is the share of trips to the airport from the ridings that are for business purposes either originating at business premises or residents travelling for business reasons. For example, the King Vaughan riding has 35% of its labour force working in management, business, finance and admin-istration occupations compared to an Ontario average of 28%. There is also a much higher incidence of self-employment in King Vaughan with 16% reporting that employment status compared to 12% in Ontario as a whole. So, this riding has a disproportionate number of managers and entrepreneurs and therefore likely a higher incidence of business travel. Measures to make ground access to Toronto Pearson faster and more

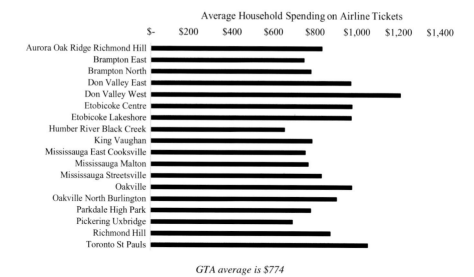

Figure 7.6 Local Economic Impacts: Propensity for Air Travel *GTA average is $774*.
Source: Statistics Canada and Greater Toronto Airports Authority.

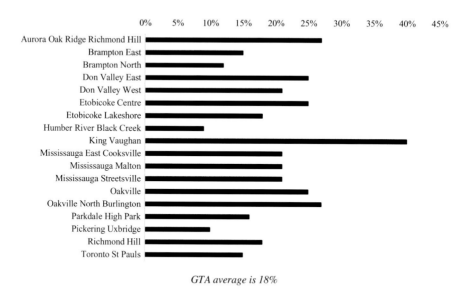

Figure 7.7 Local Economic Impacts: Supporting Business *GTA average is 18%*.
Source: Statistics Canada and Greater Toronto Airports Authority.

reliable will resonate strongly. In contrast, Humber River-Black Creek has 19% of its labour force in management, business, finance and administration occupations and 8% are self-employed, so this riding generates fewer business trips to the airport.

The ARI can be built from any number of metrics including 'issues du jour' or from a set that reflects the economic, environmental and social pillars of sustainability, for example:

- What percentage of the labour force in your electoral district is employed at the airport?
- What is the propensity for air travel by your voters?
- How important is the airport to business in your community?
- What share of passenger trips to the airport are made by public transit?

Most airports already have the data at hand to construct an Airport Relevance Index (ARI).

PRODUCTIVITY

A study[14] of US airports over a 20-year period found that the air connectivity available at the local airport feeds through into productivity improvements in the regional economy. These vary by industry and type of air connections. For example, a 10% increase in international non-stop destinations served translates into a 0.38% increase in productivity across all industries while a 10% increase in domestic destinations converts to a 0.28% productivity lift. Manufacturing companies were particularly sensitive to the number of domestic destinations served with two or more daily non-stop flights, but the finance and insurance industry saw the biggest positive impact on its productivity from the number of domestic airline hubs served non-stop. Professional and technical services were more closely linked to share of global GDP accessible from the local airport. These variations reflect the way different industries rely on air transport, for example, manufacturing is predominantly a domestic industry as the share of US economy[15] accounted for by the export of goods has averaged 8.4% since 2010. The finance and insurance sector, where 'road warriors' tend to work, prizes the frequency and choice that better hub connectivity delivers while companies in the professional services category are more likely to be operating internationally, for example, these now account for 27% of US service exports,[16] a share that has doubled over the last 20 years.

Going back to Chapter 2, the type of air network connectivity that most benefits the regional economy should inform the strategic plan.

INNOVATION

Many airports pay homage to innovation, but the industry's track record is actually very poor. In 2019, only 64 US patents were issued in the field but none to airport owners and operators, instead they went to vendors to the industry such as Honeywell and IBM. The reality is that airports, with a few exceptions, do not have the scale, focus or motivation to really drive innovation.

The World Intellectual Property Organization (WIPO) stated recently that 'it is the need for greater collaboration in the face of growing technological complexity that has driven both the increasing concentration of innovation in certain urban areas and its global spread'.[17] WIPO also report that teams now account for 80% of patents in the late 2010s up from 64% in the first decade of this century. In other words, innovation is a team sport and often a multi-national one, all of which means air travel. For example, of the just over 500 US patents issued to applicants from Vancouver, Canada in 2019, the average number of inventors per patent was 2.64, international inventors were team members in 20% of the cases and many more were pan-Canadian teams.

Probably, an airport's most important contribution to innovation is to ensure it supports the air network connectivity to enable this teamwork.

At a very basic level, innovation improves productivity which improves standards of living but more specifically it leads to better economic and social outcomes, all of which drive up the demand for air travel.

Research in the US shows that on average, a 10% increase in business travel leads to an increase in patenting by about 0.2%, and inward business travel is about one fourth as potent for innovation as domestic R&D spending.[18]

Remember the movie *Good Will Hunting*? Matt Damon is a janitor at Harvard and solves math problems left on the blackboard in the classrooms he's cleaning. Research shows that this is not entirely fictional. From the social clubs of eighteenth-century Edinburgh to the present-day Silicon Valley in California, when you get skilled and talented people in one place, you tend to get more patents, innovation and higher wages for both high skilled and low-skilled workers.

Looking at Canadian data, the innovativeness of a metropolitan area has a significant and positive impact on the economy and can explain between 10% and 20% of the variation in prosperity. All other things equal, a 10% increase in the innovation rate[19] of a Canadian metro area results in:

• a 0.4% increase in the labour force participation rate,
• a decline in the unemployment rate of 0.6%, and
• a 0.7% increase in after-tax household incomes.[20]

The impact of innovation on poverty is positive and mediated through the labour force participation rate. Specifically, a 10% increase in the innovation rate results in a 0.4% increase in labour force participation which, in turn, leads to a 6.5% reduction in the prevalence of low incomes, defined as the cut off below which an above average percentage of household income is devoted to necessities.

The basic theory is that having more smart people in one place increases innovation. For every 10% larger metropolitan area, its innovation rate increases by 5%. The quality of human capital is important too: a 10% increase in the share of the population with a university degree increases the innovation rate by 15.8%. When we drill down, it is graduates in STEM[21] subjects that are the driving force. Of the 25–64 years age group with a university degree, a 10% increase in those that studied a STEM subject results in a 28% increase in the rate of innovation.

The share of the visible minority population is positively correlated with innovation, even controlling for the big city effect.

Linking innovation back to international education, another sector enabled by the air transport industry, a 10% increase in the number of people aged 25–64 who have studied abroad, relative to population, results in an 8% increase in the innovation rate. This speaks to the professional and social networks that overseas study creates which can become crucibles for invention.

Finally, customers can be the biggest innovators. No company invented the Camelbak, the hydration device for cyclists: it was a competitive, long-distance racer in Texas, who happened to be a paramedic, who first strapped two IV bags full of water to his back. Likewise are the sports bra and baby jogger. An airport example is passengers repurposing obsolete pay-phone cabins as workstations or repurposing bits of asphalt off the airport approach roads as a cellphone parking lot. Smart companies watch, listen and learn from their customers as they adapt products to meet their actual, specific needs.

SHAPING THE ECONOMY

Finally, the airport itself then shapes the regional economy, for example, the Toronto metropolitan area was home to 17% of all jobs in Canada and 16% of jobs in transportation and warehousing in 2007 but ten years later, as shown in Figure 7.8, Toronto was now specializing in this sector and accounting for a larger share of national jobs, partly because of Pearson Airport's evolution into a global hub. In sectors dependent on aviation such as professional and technical services and finance and real estate, Toronto's share of national jobs also increased.

AUTOMATION

Finally, a word on automation. Will an airport 50 years hence have less humans working at it? Probably but every technological advance creates more new jobs than it displaces, so for all the jobs driving buses that were lost when the private automobile became ubiquitous, many more were created on assembly lines, in automobile showrooms and repair shops.

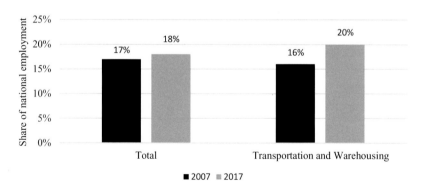

Figure 7.8 Shaping the Economy.
Source: Statistics Canada.

Some of the leading thinkers on this are at MIT[22] in Boston, MA, including Daron Acemoglu, David Autor and Erik Brynjolfsson. A key insight they offer is that jobs do not get automated, tasks do and tasks can be subdivided into routine and non-routine and manual and cognitive. For example, a routine manual task would be repetitive assembly while a non-routine, cognitive task would be legal drafting.[23] Automation is making inroads into the non-routine tasks including the cognitive ones. For example, it is now not uncommon for the first round of job interviews to be conducted by a computer.

Another comprehensive report[24] from the University of Oxford estimates the probability of automation in various occupational categories. The report identifies high, medium and low risk occupations and estimates that around 47% of total US employment is in the high-risk category including transportation and logistics occupations, office and administrative support workers and production occupations. No time frame is stated for the process, although we can expect it to be non-linear and there are many variables involved including the relative cost of capital and labour, government policy, industrial relations and the airport's strategy and brand. For example, given the high incidence of mobility impairments in an aging population, more non-routine, cognitive tasks may materialize.

It would be reasonable to infer that many occupations with a high probability of automation are found disproportionately at airports. When we look at the occupational breakdown of jobs, shown in Figure 7.9, at

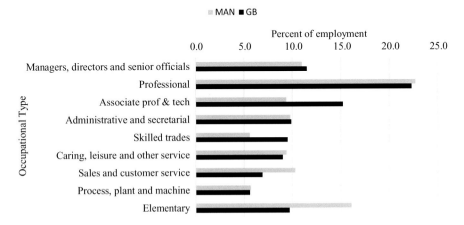

Figure 7.9 Occupational Characteristics at Manchester Airport.
Source: UK Office of National Statistics.

Manchester Airport (MAN) in the UK, as an example, compared to the national average, we see the airport has a higher share of elementary, process, plant and machine and sales and customer service jobs, all of which are more likely to be automated.

We see similar patterns at Sydney Airport (SYD), shown in Figure 7.10, where occupations with a high probability of automation such as manual labour and the operation of machinery and equipment are prevalent.

SUMMARY AND CONCLUSIONS

Airports generate, enable and shape economic activity, all of which can be captured, analysed and reported. To build social licence, and political support, these numbers provide invaluable context for on-going operations and major expansion projects.

The traditional economic impact metrics of jobs, taxes and GDP only tell part of the story. In any event, this approach is facing a number of challenges including declining participation and stalled out total job numbers due to the consolidation of air carriers and other factors.

Airports need to move beyond their boundaries and understand the catalytic or wider impacts that arise from opening up new export markets for businesses, enabling innovation and increasing the productivity of

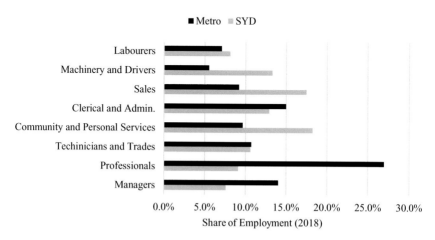

Figure 7.10 Occupational Characteristics at Sydney Airport.

Source: Australian Bureau of Statistics.

the regional economy. These can be very powerful advocacy tools, if communicated as narratives rather than in dry, abstract statistics.

An airport's economic impact can be customized at a national, regional and local level, all of which increases the size of the audience and by tailoring it, the effectiveness of the message.

Going forward, assessing the economic impact of airports will be less of a numbers game but focused more on job quality and outcomes for targeted groups such as young people or low-income neighbourhoods or particular industries or trends such as innovation.

Many airports pay homage to innovation but the industry's track record is actually very poor. However, given that innovation is increasingly a multi-national team sport, supporting air network connectivity is the key contribution of airports.

Airports have a disproportionate number of jobs with a high probability of automation and while the timing and trajectory are uncertain, we would expect to see less employment at airports for a given passenger and cargo volume in the decades ahead, although this will be leavened by the airport's brand, needs of its customers and novel products and services that will emerge.

. . . .

Notes

1. $R = 0.80$.
2. For example, 1,000 taxi and TNC trips to and from the airport per day of an average duration of 0.75 hours is 750 person hours of employment per day or 273,750 person hours per year which, at an average of 1,700 person hours per job, equals 161 person years of employment.
3. A general rule here is to attribute hotel employment to the airport based on the number of room nights from flight crew and passengers staying overnight between, before or after flights.
4. Indirect and induced jobs can easily be double the number of direct jobs.
5. This is room for debate here but generally only taxes on tickets originating at the airport should be included.
6. In this case, it is important to capture all the employments at the airport, not just that directly related to on-going operations. Suppose the air traffic control organization has its training centre at the airport and there are 500 students and employees working there. These would not be considered jobs associated with the on-going operation of the airport but the trips generated need to be factored into ground access planning.
7. A good rule of thumb is that 75% of airport employees possess a security badge, so numbers can be prorated up accordingly.

8. These comparisons are easily done by looking at line items in government budgets.
9. Defined as direct jobs at Pearson per capita based Forward Sortation Area population and on airport security pass numbers issued to addresses in that FSA with an adjustment for airport employees without a pass.
10. For convenience, we used the FSAs identified by the Government of Ontario for Covid-19 vaccination priority as a surrogate for low-income neighbourhoods.
11. McGrath, *Seeing around Corners.*
12. The difference between what non-residents are paying air carriers and airports in these countries and what residents of those countries are buying from foreign air carriers and airports.
13. I can confirm that this is fine. All we'd ask is that an acknowledgement is included as to where the content was first published, along with the journal's website; Brown, "The Airport Relevance Index".
14. Gillen, Landau, and Gosling "Measuring the Relationship", 66–75.
15. U.S. Bureau of Economic Analysis, "Shares of Gross Domestic Product".
16. U.S. Bureau of Economic Analysis, "International Trade in Goods and Services".
17. WIPO, "The Geography of Innovation".
18. Hovhannisyan and Keller, "International Business Travel", 75–104.
19. Defined as US patents awarded per capita.
20. An incidental benefit is that the positive impact on household income stimulates spending on airline tickets. In Vancouver, a 10% increase in household income translates into a 5.7% increase in spending on airline tickets for leisure and personal trips.
21. Science, technology, engineering and mathematics.
22. Massachusetts Institute of Technology, Boston, MA.
23. Autor, Levy, and Murnane, "The Skill Content", 1279–1333.
24. Frey and Osborne, "The Future of Employment".

Bibliography

Autor, David H., Frank Levy, and Richard J. Murnane. "The Skill Content of Recent Technological Change: An Empirical Exploration". *The Quarterly Journal of Economics* 118, no. 4 (November 2003): 1279–1333. https://doi.org/10.1162/003355303322552801.

Brown, Mike. "The Airport Relevance Index: A New Tool for Advocacy and Influence – The Case of Toronto Pearson International Airport". *Journal of Airport Management* 15, no. 4 (September 2021): https://www.henrystewartpublications.com/jam.

Frey, Carl Benedikt, and Michael A. Osborne. *The Future of Employment: How Susceptible Are Jobs to Computerisation*. Oxford, Oxford Martin Programme on Technology and Employment, 2013.

Gillen, David, Steven Landau, and Geoffrey D. Gosling. "Measuring the Relationship between Airline Network Connectivity and Productivity". *Transportation Research Record: Journal of the Transportation Research Board* 2501, no. 1 (January 2015): 66–75. https://doi.org/10.3141/2501-09.

Hovhannisyan, Nune, and Wolfgang Keller. "International Business Travel: An Engine of Innovation?" *Journal of Economic Growth* 20 (2015): 75–104. https://doi.org/10.1007/s10887-014-9107-7.

McGrath, Rita. *Seeing around Corners: How to Spot Inflection Points in Business Before They Happen*. New York, NY, Houghton Mifflin Harcourt, 2019.

U.S. Bureau of Economic Analysis. "International Trade in Goods and Services".

U.S. Bureau of Economic Analysis. "Shares of Gross Domestic Product: Exports of Goods, FRED, Federal Reserve Bank of St. Louis". Updated January 28, 2021. https://fred.stlouisfed.org/series/A253RE1A156NBEA.

World Intellectual Property Report 2019 – The Geography of Innovation: Local Hotspots, Global Networks, World Intellectual Property Organization, Geneva, 2019. World Intellectual Property Report 2019 – The Geography of Innovation: Local Hotspots, Global Networks (wipo.int).

8

LOOKING AHEAD

INTRODUCTION

As the famous strategist Mike Tyson once said, 'everybody has a plan until they get smacked in the face'. These punches can be in the form of long-term structural trends such as concern about climate change or sudden ones like the Covid-19 pandemic. What does the future hold in terms of disruption and innovation? This chapter will offer some simple frameworks to think about these contemporary issues ... and a history lesson.

ONE HUNDRED YEARS AGO

When we think about how the air transport industry recovers from Covid-19, the changes in technology and business models already underway and climate change, there is a parallel, and possibly a parable, from how the Spanish Flu affected the dominant intercity mode of passenger transportation of the day, the railway.

It never recovered.

We will use Canada as our case study and acknowledge that the experience of other countries may have been different. The Spanish Flu pandemic of 1918–1919 killed about 50,000 Canadians out of a total population of 8 million. It also disproportionately struck the young and able-bodied ... and this after 60,000 Canadians died in World War I. There were three waves: Spring 1918, Fall 1918 and Winter 1919. To date, Covid-19 has killed 25,000 Canadians[1] on a population of 37 million.

The first, striking parallel is that rail travel and air travel both saw strong growth in the ten years before the pandemic with CAGRs[2] of 3.9% and 4.5%, respectively, as shown in Figure 8.1. Canadian airports had their best ten years in the decade before Covid-19 as did Canada's

 DOI: 10.4324/9781003173267-8

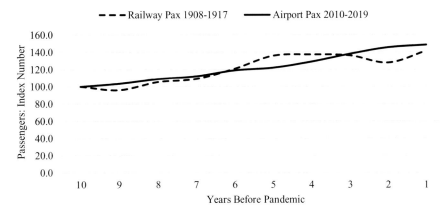

Figure 8.1 Pre-Pandemic Trends in Rail and Air Travel.

Source: Canada, Dominion Bureau of Statistics, Canada Year Books and Author's Calculations.

railways 100 years ago and the real surge in rail travel occurred in 1912 and 1913 before the start of World War I.

Railway passenger volumes in Canada never recovered to pre-pandemic levels. By 1938, Canada's railroads were serving less than half the customers they did in 1918 due to economic forces and technological change.

The Canadian economy went into a recession in 1921 and then the Great Depression hit in the 1930s, but the number of motor vehicles registered in Canada increased by 500% in the 20 years from the end of World War I, as illustrated in Figures 8.2 and 8.3. When you read the history, you can infer that the customer experience as a railway passenger

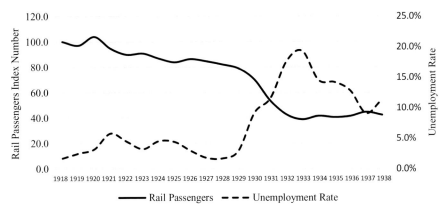

Figure 8.2 Economic Factors Affecting Rail Demand.

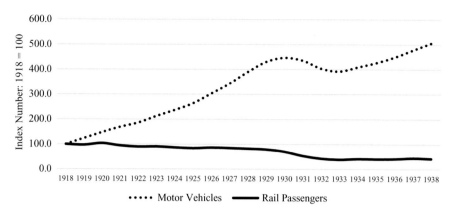

Figure 8.3 Technological Factors Affecting Rail Demand.

Source: Canada, Dominion Bureau of Statistics, Canada Year Books and Author's Calculations.

was not the greatest as the industry was beset with strikes, mergers and bankruptcies and we do not know for sure but the privacy of an automobile, the ability to travel with your own 'bubble' to use the current parlance, may have been even more attractive after the pandemic.

When we model the roles of technological disruption and economic conditions in explaining the decline in rail travel after the Spanish Flu, the motor vehicle was a more important factor than the economy.

What will be the disruptions affecting the structural demand for air travel after Covid-19? Zoom and Skype? 'Uber Air'? De-globalization? Climate change? And, what will be the trajectory of the economy after the pandemic? Jeff Bezos, former CEO of Amazon, is quoted as saying 'People don't have any idea yet how impactful the Internet is going to be and that this is still Day 1 in such a big way',[3] so it's reasonable to surmise that there are technological opportunities and challenges coming at us that we may only be able to dimly foresee. For example, the Internet of Things (IOT) could revolutionize asset maintenance with advanced AI technologies that can create exact digital replicas of airports to plan, model, design and manage and operate more efficiently.

COVID-19 PANDEMIC RECOVERY

The aviation industry has been put in the equivalent of a medically induced coma while we collectively fight Covid-19. It's a time of extraordinary challenges but also opportunities. These 'Black Swan' events can be rocket fuel for innovation, accelerate social changes already underway, for example, on-line shopping and working from home (WFH) but also spawn new businesses like Uber which started in the depths of the Great Financial Crisis in 2009, Microsoft which emerged in 1975 after the oil price shock and Disney in 1923, in the aftermath of our last pandemic, the Spanish Flu.

In terms of frameworks for building demand recovery scenarios, think about a four-layer cake in which we consider the cyclical and structural response to Covid-19 as a series of concentric rings moving out from the industry itself to broader society and economy.

1. What would the 'business as usual' trajectory look like? In other words, start with a simplifying assumption that the basic relationships between the demand for air travel and economy and society will return to pre-pandemic levels and assess what the recovery trajectory could look like on that basis.
2. Then, layer in a set of reasonable assumptions about how the pandemic may have altered these relationships. For example, the cost of air travel will increase because of quarantine, pre- and post-flight testing, lower aircraft utilization rates due to sanitation protocols or a consumer preference for non-stop flights to avoid the additional touchpoints at a connecting airport. For example, passengers may be prepared to pay a premium for non-stop service even though it may only operate four days a week.
3. Moving to the realm of structural change, the question is how much business and leisure air travel will permanently migrate to 'virtual', and if the front of the plane is empty, then fares at the back will have increased, depressing demand, not to mention the sheer discomfort of having to wear a mask for hours on end.
4. The final layer is a consideration of broader societal trends such as concern that may dampen the demand, for example, air transport's GHG emissions, role as a 'virus vector' or de-globalization. Having been locked down and staying local, will our values change so that less social status attaches to international travel?

Of course, there is no 'right' answer but the process outlined above will at least ensure a systematic consideration of the issues and we are looking for a net number here, after the pent-up demand has been sated. The lesson from the Spanish Flu was that it was the emergence of the automobile that contributed more to the decline of rail travel than economic conditions which suggests that layers (3) and (4) deserve more attention than (1) and (2).

CLIMATE CHANGE

There are many excellent, in-depth studies on the role of aviation in climate change. The intention is not to replicate them here but rather summarize the 'state of play'. The good news is that aviation can achieve net zero emissions by 2050 using technologies that already exist or are in sight.

The IPCC[4] has stated that for limiting global warming to 1.5 °C to avoid the worst outcomes that climate change could visit upon us, global CO_2 emissions must fall to net zero by around 2050. Under a pre-pandemic 'business-as-usual' scenario, aviation carbon emissions would rise by 83% by 2050. By the way, 'net zero' means what it says, that is, a sector really is at zero emissions and not because it buys carbon credits and offsets from another sector.

The three paths are: improving efficiency, demand management and decarbonization.

- Aircrafts have become significantly more fuel efficient and there is no indication that this trend will not continue as airlines relentlessly reduce costs, especially if there is a permanent loss of some business travel post Covid-19. It's not just engine technology but improvements in air traffic control that permit more direct routings. Airports can help by building and operating efficient airfields that minimize taxi-times and delays on the ground.
- Demand management, for example, carbon taxes could cut aviation emissions by 15%. Another example is that, as a condition of bailing out Air France, the French government has told the airline to stop flying short-haul routes when high-speed rail is an alternative.
- The heavy lifting needed to get aviation to net zero by 2050 will have to be done by decarbonization. In addition to changes in material and aircraft design, this means powering aircraft in new ways, for example, with electricity or bio-aviation fuels. Hydrogen may have a role to play too as well as hybrids. Different categories of aircraft, corporate, passenger and freight will evolve in different ways and at different rates but with mutations and adaptation between them. Of course, with an average aircraft lifespan of 25–30 years, it will take time for fundamental changes in aircraft design and propulsion to work their way into the fleet.

Kerosene is the pre-eminent aviation fuel because of its unique weight to power ratio. That is, it's light enough for a plane to be able to take off with a profitable payload of passengers and cargo but its enormous energy punch means that plane can fly from Los Angeles to Sydney. The good news is that we can create synthetic or plant-based kerosene known as bio-aviation fuel (BAF) which is an identical twin chemically and can be pumped through our current aviation fuel infrastructure and into the existing aircraft fleet. One of the concerns about biofuels is that we end up generating as many emissions producing and transporting them as we would burning kerosene. However, this is not the case with BAF from forest residue.

The weight to power ratio for electric aircraft presents challenges in that the batteries needed to fly to London mean the aircraft probably could not get off the ground, let alone carry any passengers or cargo. However, electric power does have the potential to propel short-haul flights. The decarbonization stars align when there is a lot of short-haul flying and abundant sources of green electricity.

Biofuels are currently between two and eight times more expensive than traditional kerosene. We will need a policy and regulatory framework to ensure suppliers of biofuels have a market to sell to, for example, by mandating a certain percentage in the fuel mix that would increase over time. This could be an opportune moment with politicians supporting green-infrastructure recovery plans and near zero interest rates.

Although it's a relatively small share of GHG emissions compared to aircraft manoeuvring around an airport, decarbonizing ground access will take place through the natural evolution of the personal vehicle fleet to lower emission engines but further improvements to public transit access to airports will be helpful. Discouraging passenger drop-off and pick-up because of the dead-head component of such trips will be in the playbook too.[5]

Is this concern about the GHG emissions from aviation causing consumers to change their behaviour? To gauge public sentiment, Internet search activity can be helpful. Looking at several search terms that might capture this concern such as 'climate emergency', 'flight shaming' and 'air travel carbon' reveal that interest was pretty stable from 2013 to the beginning in 2019, when it increased dramatically partly because of the high profile given to the issue by the young, Swedish campaigner, Greta Thunberg, as Figure 8.4 shows.

Globally, the impact on demand is barely perceptible with a 10% increase in Internet search activity for 'air travel carbon', as a proxy for public disquiet translating into a 0.05% reduction in demand.[6] However, in regions that have experienced extreme weather, and the consequences of it, such as wildfires in California and Australia the impacts on demand are greater, as Table 8.1 shows.

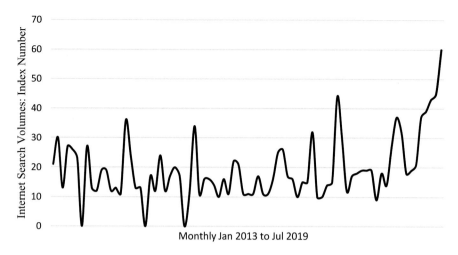

Figure 8.4 Public Interest in Carbon Emissions Associated with Air Travel.
Source: Google Trends.

Table 8.1 The 'Greta Effect' Concern about Climate Change and Impact on Demand for Air Travel

A 10% Increase in Internet Searches for	Country/State	Percentage change in passengers
'GHG'	Sweden	−0.7
'Air Travel Carbon'	Australia	−0.6
'Air Travel Carbon'	California	−0.7

Source: Author's calculation of data from Google Trends, Commonwealth of Australia, US Bureau of Transportation Statistics, Swedavia.
Notes: Percentage change in passengers is, respectively, for EU passengers at Swedish airports, total Australian airport passengers and passengers at LAX and SFO.

What is striking is that the coefficient is directionally correct and very similar in three different jurisdictions. The impact is not, yet, large which we would expect given how embedded air travel is in our lives, that is, change is not going to happen overnight. Notably, the market most affected in Sweden is air travel within the EU for which there are reasonable substitutes like high-speed rail.

In terms of physical planning, factors to consider include longer runways to maintain aircraft performance in hotter summers, changes in flight times due to more intense head and tail winds, higher risks from extreme weather events impairing operations and infrastructure and the effect of sea level rise on coastal airports.

DISRUPTION

Disruption is arguably an overused word but nonetheless captures the scale and speed at which existing businesses are being re-made. In some cases, this is because of a new technology such as the iPod rendering the CD obsolete or a new platform such as Airbnb which does not own a single hotel room, nor does Uber own any cars, but both have transformed their industries.

According to Clay Christensen of Harvard Business School who developed the original concept of disruption, the strict definition is a company that enters the market with a product or service that's inferior to that of the incumbent but that is 'good enough'. The classic example is Toyota entering the US market in the 1960s with boxy little cars that were not as good as a Ford or Chevrolet but were 'good enough' for students and homemakers looking for a little runabout. Fast forward 40 years and Toyota is the world's largest automobile manufacturer with Ford and General Motors ranked fourth and seventh, respectively. What happens is that the disruptor starts by taking the bottom end of the market from the incumbent who surrenders that territory on the grounds that it was a low yield segment anyway. The problem for the incumbent is the disruptor then steadily moves up the food chain and is soon producing regular and high-end brands. Incumbents recognize what is happening but rationally they focus on improving their products for their best and most profitable customers, often to the point of overcomplicating them, as anybody who has struggled with the heating controls in a new automobile can attest. In Chapter 2, we cited some examples of air carriers creating low-cost subsidiaries to compete with disruptive new entrants, with very little success.

Most people would agree that business meetings or family gatherings by way of video conference are inferior to assembling in person, but they may be good enough in a lot of cases. We can reasonably assume that video meeting technology gets better and cheaper while air travel should see fewer restrictions and inconveniences, but there will be the ever-present risk of a sudden lockdown or ban on flights from a hotspot country and wearing a mask for ten hours is not pleasant. Is 'virtual' to aviation was what the automobile was to the railways after the Spanish Flu?

INTANGIBLE ASSETS

Assets were essentially the focus of Chapters 4 and 5 but these were physical ones: runways, terminal buildings and roads. However,

Jonathan Haskel, of Imperial College, London and Stian Westlake wrote a seminal book in 2018 entitled *Capitalism without Capital: The Rise of the Intangible Economy*. A company's intangible assets are the ones you cannot see or touch and include design, brand, R&D, software and networks. They cite research that found that Microsoft's traditional assets of plant and equipment were only worth $3 billion, equivalent to 4% of its total assets and 1% of its market value.

Compared to physical ones, intangible assets have different characteristics, namely, scalability, sunkenness, spillovers and synergies (the 'Four Ss'):

- *Scalability*: physical assets can only be used in one place and at one time while intangible assets can be used repeatedly and in multiple places.
- *Sunkenness* involves irrecoverable costs, and when it comes to intangible assets, because they tend to be very context specific or unique to the company, its brand and operating system. If Tim Hortons, a Canadian coffee and baked goods chain, went bankrupt, some money could be recovered from the tables, chairs and coffee machines but that would not come close to the value of the brand or its 'always fresh' logistics system.
- *Spillovers* are often created by intangible investments, and it is relatively easy for other businesses, including competitors, to take advantage of these in a way which tends to discourage R&D. If you own a taxi company, it is very difficult for a competitor to sneak into your depot at night and use your taxis but that is not the case with an idea.
- *Synergies* are important in intangible-based economies, as ideas often work well together. The concept of 'open innovation', defined as when a firm imports new knowledge from outside the company, is a major driver of intangible synergies at both the company and industry levels, as well as for the national and local economies. For example, the microwave oven started off as a defence research project, but after a series of happy accidents that revealed it could heat food, it was only when Raytheon bought a kitchen appliance manufacturer that it became a ubiquitous household item.

SUMMARY AND CONCLUSIONS

This chapter has only been a summary of some of the main trends, but others include the potential of machine learning and Artificial Intelligence. For example, modelling the flooding patterns of a river requires millions of data points that we have not up until now had the capacity to analyse quickly and comprehensively. Now we can and it will allow affected airports to prepare and mitigate more effectively. Another trend is unmanned aerial vehicles (UAVs) including drones. For airports, there are many implications; on the one hand, the malicious deployment of drones can cripple operations, but on the other hand, they also have great potential to inspect runways and monitor the security perimeter.

Notes

1. As of May 11, 2021.
2. Compound annual growth rate.
3. Stone, "The Everything Store: Jeff Bezos and the Age of Amazon".
4. Intergovernmental Panel on Climate Change.
5. Miyoshi and Mason, "The Damage Cost of Carbon Dioxide", 137–143.
6. At a selected group of global hub airports: AMS, CDG, HKG, LAX, LHR, MUC, SFO, SYD and YYZ.

Bibliography

Haskel, Jonathan and Westlake, Stian. *Capitalism without Capital: The Rise of the Intangible Economy.* Oxford, Princeton University Press, 2018.

Miyoshi, Chikage, and Keith J. Mason. "The Damage Cost of Carbon Dioxide Emissions Produced by Passengers on Airport Surface Access: The Case of Manchester Airport". *Journal of Transport Geography* 28 (April 2013): 137–143. https://doi.org/10.1016/j.jtrangeo.2012.12.003.

Stone, Brad, *The Everything Store: Jeff Bezos and the Age of Amazon.* New York, Little, Brown and Company, 2013.

9

SUMMARY AND CONCLUSIONS

OVERVIEW

This book has argued that airport planning has never been more challenging, nor more important. The capital intensity of the business means that investments have long incubation periods, and they are infrequent, immovable, inalienable and come with externalities; yet the rules of the game are changing as society tackles climate change, technological change speeds ahead and business models get disrupted. And, this was before the Covid-19 pandemic. Essentially, airport planning is a risk management exercise designed to minimize the danger of sub-optimal investments and loss of social license. The antidote, the book argues, is to move airport planning beyond its traditional boundaries, outside its comfort zone if you like, by adopting new concepts, frameworks and methods.

An analogy is to think of traditional airport planning as characterized by straight lines. Demand forecasts are linear, and they get translated into facilities and land uses by fixed coefficients. 'New' airport planning is however all about curves, specifically, the next inflection point, and how strategy, technology and business models make the translation into capacity more sinuous.

Several themes run through the book. One is that change is non-linear, whether we are talking about demand, consumer preference, technologies or business models and understanding where you are on the S-curve, and timing of and vector off the next inflection point, is key. A second is that the boundaries between 'on-airport' and 'off-airport' are blurring geographically and functionally. A third is the concept of the 'trilemma' which is where of three possible outcomes, only two are achievable and failing to recognize that this is the root cause of many blunt and ineffective strategies.

DOI: 10.4324/9781003173267-9

Conceptually, this leads to thinking about planning airports as component of larger systems. Any transportation system is comprised of three components: terminals, vehicles and the 'way'. Changes in one can add or detract value from other. For example, the advances in aircraft engine technology and air traffic procedures that led to ETOPS[1] adversely affected the fortunes of some airports while boosting others. Another system is the regional economy in which an airport responds to, generates, enables, attracts and shapes economic activity. For example, when an airport invests in infrastructure to make itself more competitive as a global hub, it improves the productivity of certain sectors of the economy and alters land values and uses for many miles beyond its perimeter. System planning helps us to identify, anticipate and understand these effects and the stakeholders involved.

STEP-BY-STEP

Chapter 1 introduced the concept of a Pyramid of Planning with strategy at the top and cascading down through a series of plans of increasing granularity down to this year's operating plan and budget. The interlinked layers of planning in the Pyramid are intended to minimize the risk of misalignment or discontinuity between the strategy and the day-to-day running of an airport. Many forces are at work to break this chain, the urgent taking precedence over the important (recognizing that there are real emergencies that need attending to), powerful constituencies with different agendas or simply a miscommunication or misunderstanding of the bigger picture.

Without a clear and unambiguous strategy, the dependent plans in the Pyramid will necessarily be weak, yet it is at strategic planning that many airports get tangled up in a mixture of good intentions, emotive language ('to be the best airport in…') and virtue signalling. Chapter 2 sets out a series of templates to ensure that the strategic plan responds to the real challenges and opportunities presenting themselves including a systematic assessment of the competitive forces acting upon an airport. Key concepts are identifying and resolving 'trilemmas' wherein an airport tries to pursue three outcomes when only two are possible, captured by the old business expression: 'fast, cheap or good: pick two'. Other principles are focusing strategy on solving a real problem, not just making noble statements, and that potential perturbations first appear as shallow ripples at the edges of the enterprise but can end up being breakers.

The main takeaway from Chapter 3 on demand forecasting is that change is non-linear and we need to be wary of straight-line forecasts. A time series of demand almost always resembles an S-curve, and the critical task is determining the timing of and the vector off the next inflection. Any number of factors can cause an inflection: change in air carrier strategy, bi-lateral air policy, the capabilities of aircraft engines, air traffic control procedures, exchange rates and tourist visa policy, even the airport's own strategy, have all caused airports' growth rates to inflect. The analogy used is that a linear forecast is like the base of a soup, necessary but not especially tasty or nourishing but when inflection points are added, it becomes a more appetizing stew. Mixing in probabilities of outcomes is like throwing croutons on top. Finally, the potential of Big Data, in terms of how it reveals true customer preference and interest, is demonstrated.

Chapter 4 sets out how to best match passenger demand with capacity in which there are two sub-processes. The first is to understand that the coefficients by which we translate demand into capacity are dynamic, due to advances in technology and changes in customer preferences. For example, airport terminal planners in many cases missed the S-curve transition from in-terminal check-in to on-line while airside planners failed to appreciate just how successfully air carriers would deploy bigger planes and fill more seats on them, deferring the need for new runway capacity. The second part of the process, having determined that new capacity is needed, is deciding what and where to build it. There are many traps here including the 'favourite' or 'obvious' option but this sometimes does not survive a forensic examination of its performance against a wide-ranging set of evaluation criteria. A disciplined and deliberative process here can reveal new options and hybrids as well as engage business partners, stakeholders, and the community. Deviating from a Master Plan is sometimes warranted due to a material change in circumstances or indeed a refinement of the strategy but more often, it is a tactical decision to capitalize on financially attractive development proposal or to sub-optimally locate a facility to reduce short-run servicing costs. Inevitably, the long-run costs outweigh the immediate benefits, so having robust processes in place to deliberate on these issues is important. Finally, some sense checks are offered in terms of an airport's asset base relative to its traffic and injecting the customer into the planning process, a good thing, by showing how on-time performance and asset base can be optimized.

Cargo is often glossed over but the pandemic has shown how important airports are in the delivery of PPE and vaccines, and it has been a more resilient business than passengers. The seismic shift to on-line shopping induced by the pandemic further reinforces the point. Chapter 5 points out that air cargo is a more agile and volatile business and in the universe of freight, and value-to-weight ratios, it is lobster to the basmati rice of rail freight or the ground coffee of truck transportation. The sizing and location of cargo facilities are very sensitive to assumptions about such things as the level of automation and exclusive versus common use business models, and because minutes matter for integrated carriers like FedEx or DHL, the siting of their facilities needs to be a fine-grained exercise. In other words, cargo is a riskier and more demanding proposition for airports which is possibly why it has not been a central focus for many of them. Yet, in terms of an airport's bottom-line, economic impact and social licence, cargo is arguably becoming more important.

Chapters 7 and 8 move the conversation beyond the traditional boundaries of the airport in terms of their geographic and economic impacts.

In Chapter 7, we see that airports are magnets and businesses, and people with a high propensity to fly tend to locate close to them; in fact, the wealthiest neighbourhood in any city tends to be 30 minutes' drive to the airport, so close enough but not too close. After controlling for size, type and age of building and other local effects, commercial property values increase with proximity to an airport. When the quality of ground access improves, that is, it becomes faster and more reliable with the construction of a rail link to the airport, there is a further uplift in values. Yet, many airports are only dimly aware of the fact that they are lining the pockets of landlords, and the governments that tax them, by virtue of their investment in the airport in general and ground access in particular. Although not impossible, there are many theoretical and practical challenges to capturing this value uplift, or some portion of it, but at the very least, it should be credited to the airport's economic impact account. In the opposite direction, by sticking to old noise exposure contours that do not reflect advances in aircraft and air navigation technology, airports may be sterilizing land for residential development, and providing some relief if housing affordability is an issue. Equally, the old notion that the airport should only host aviation-related uses is not helpful any longer; we should talk about aviation dependent land uses instead, which would allow a just-in-time manufacturer shipping and receiving daily by air closer to the airport than service centres where car rental companies repair and rotate their fleets. Urban form is 'sticky', so it can take decades to adjust to a new equilibrium but the case for integrated planning of the airport and the area around it is compelling, to deliver higher returns for everyone.

The economic impact of an airport discussed in Chapter 8 is so much more than the number of jobs, amount of taxes and contribution to GDP from ongoing operations but this is sometimes the limit of an airport's ambition. The link back to an airport's strategy is that the economic structure of the region it serves will profit from certain types of air services more than others. For example, the productivity of domestically oriented manufacturers relies on connectivity to national hubs but where IT dominates it is the share of global GDP accessible that boosts competitiveness. This is where we get into the territory of wider, or catalytic, economic impacts and narratives around them like how cherries from British Columbia, Canada find their way into the supermarkets in Hong Kong and China in time for Harvest Festival. Talking about a runway extension to remove vulnerability in the supply chain of local exports is much more effective in building public and political support than a ream of dry economic statistics. Another link back to strategy is building social licence by demonstrating how the airport creates jobs for under-privileged communities, targets groups such as young people and focuses more on the quality than the quantity of jobs. The latter point is particularly relevant since many tasks at airports have a high probability of automation, so reconstituting residual and emerging tasks into new jobs is a transition ahead.

Concluding Remarks

This book has been written in the middle of the Covid-19 pandemic which has seen passenger traffic essentially evaporate; the recovery trajectory is unclear and the shape of the industry afterwards is the subject of much debate. A framework for thinking about this is that airports will have to come back cleaner, greener, leaner and keener which will require strategies to be reset and new targets to be established. At the very least, thinking beyond the boundaries of airport planning will be not only desirable but also necessary because we will be in uncharted territory and will need to borrow some roadmaps.

Hopefully, this book will be of some assistance in that process.

Note

1. Extended-range Twin-engine Operations Performance Standards which essentially allow aircraft to fly across large bodies of water.

INDEX

Note: **Bold** page numbers refer to tables; *italic* page numbers refer to figures.